DISCARD

The Pacific Islands

The Pacific Islands

The Pacific Islands

Anne Wallace Sharp

LUCENT
BOOKS®

THOMSON

GALE

San Diego • Detroit • New York • San Francisco • Cleveland • New Haven, Conn. • Waterville, Maine • London • Munich

LIBRARY OF CONGRESS CATALOGING-IN-PUBLICATION DATA

Sharp, Anne Wallace,
    The pacific islands / by Anne Wallace Sharp.
    p. cm. — (Indigenous Peoples of the World)
    Summary: Discusses the history, geography, and culture of the Pacific Islands.
    Topics include: traditions, family, community, colonialism, religion, everyday
    life, and the future.
    Includes bibliographical references and index.
        ISBN 1-59018-094-1 (hardback : alk. paper)
        1. Pacific Islanders—Juvenile literature. I. Title. II. Indigenous peoples of the world
(San Diego, Calif.) III. Series.
        GN662 .S45 2003
        306'.08'09142—dc21
                                                                                2002006018

Contents

Foreword

Nearly every area of the world has indigenous populations, those people who are descended from the original settlers of a given region, often arriving many millennia ago. Many of these populations exist today despite overwhelming odds against their continuing survival.

Though indigenous populations have come under attack for a variety of reasons, in most cases land lies at the heart of the conflict. The hunger for land has threatened indigenous societies throughout history, whether the aggressor was a neighboring tribe or a foreign culture. The reason for this is simple: For indigenous populations, *way of life* has nearly always depended on the land and its bounty. Indeed, cultures from the Inuit of the frigid Arctic to the Yanomami of the torrid Amazon rain forest have been indelibly shaped by the climate and geography of the regions they inhabit.

As newcomers moved into already settled areas of the world, competition led to tension and violence. When newcomers possessed some important advantage—greater numbers or more powerful weapons—the results were predictable. History is rife with examples of outsiders triumphing over indigenous populations. Anglo-Saxons and Vikings, for instance, moved into eastern Europe and the British Isles at the expense of the indigenous Celts. Europeans traveled south through Africa and into Australia displacing the indigenous Bushmen and Aborigines while other Westerners ventured into the Pacific at the expense of the indigenous Melanesians, Micronesians, and Polynesians. And in North and South America, the colonization of the New World by European powers resulted in the decimation and displacement of numerous Native American groups.

Nevertheless, many indigenous populations retained their identity and managed to survive. Only in the last one hundred years, however, have anthropologists begun to study with any objectivity the hundreds of indigenous societies found throughout the world. And only within the last few decades have these societies been truly appreciated and acknowledged for their richness and complexity. The ability to adapt to and manage their environments is but one marker of the incredible resourcefulness of many indigenous populations. The Inuit, for example, created two distinct modes of travel for getting around the barren, icy region that is their home. The sleek, speedy kayak—with its whalebone frame and sealskin cover—allowed the Inuit to silently skim the waters of the nearby ocean and bays. And the sledge (or dogsled)—with its caribou hide platform and runners built from whalebone or frozen fish covered with sealskin—made travel over the snow- and ice-covered landscape possible.

The Indigenous Peoples of the World series strives to present a clear and realistic picture of the world's many and varied native cultures. The series captures the uniqueness as well as the similarities of indigenous societies by examining family and community life, traditional spirituality and religion, warfare, adaptation to the environment, and interaction with other native and nonnative peoples.

The series also offers perspective on the effects of Western civilization on indigenous populations as well as a multifaceted view of contemporary life. Many indigenous societies, for instance, struggle today with poverty, unemployment, racism, poor health, and a lack of educational opportunities. Others find themselves embroiled in political instability, civil unrest, and violence. Despite the problems facing these societies, many indigenous populations have regained a sense of pride in them-

selves and their heritage. Many also have experienced a resurgence of traditional art and culture as they seek to find a place for themselves in the modern world.

The Indigenous Peoples of the World series offers an in-depth study of different regions of the world and the people who have long inhabited those regions. All books in the series include fully documented primary and secondary source quotations that enliven the text. Sidebars highlight notable events, personalities, and traditions, while annotated bibliographies offer ideas for future research. Numerous maps and photographs provide the reader with a pictorial glimpse of each society.

From the Aborigines of Australia to the various indigenous peoples of the Caribbean, Europe, South America, Mexico, Asia, and Africa, the series covers a multitude of societies and their cultures. Each book stands alone and the series as a collection offers valuable comparisons of the past history and future problems of the indigenous peoples of the world.

Isolated Lands

Throughout history, islands have held a special place in the human heart. Sitting in the middle of vast oceans, these isolated and remote places have frequently stirred mankind's spirit with their hints of mystery and romance. Nowhere are such images of "paradise on earth" more applicable than in the tropical islands of the vast Pacific Ocean.

The Pacific Ocean is by far the deepest and biggest of all the world's oceans. It occupies more than one-third of the planet's surface and contains nearly twenty-five thousand different islands, the majority of which are uninhabited. Less than 2 percent of the Pacific Ocean area is land—the rest is ocean. According to the editors of National Geographic Books, "so isolated are most of [the] islands that from late 1520 to early 1521, [Spanish explorer] Ferdinand Magellan traversed some 9,000 miles from South America through the heart of Polynesia and saw only two islands."[1]

Island Groups

Historians and scholars generally divide the tropical Pacific into three main areas: Melanesia, Polynesia, and Micronesia.

Melanesia means the "black islands," and its name comes from two Greek words: *melas* which means "black" and *nesoi* meaning "islands." Early European explorers used the word "Melanesian" to describe the dark-skinned indigenous people. The islands of Melanesia are spread over a vast area of ocean and lie north and east of Australia and south of the equator. Some of the islands included in this grouping are New Guinea, New Caledonia, Fiji, Vanuatu (formerly known as New Hebrides), and the Solomons. Fiji is generally considered the dividing point between Melanesia and the rest of the Pacific.

Micronesia lies north of Melanesia and, with few exceptions, also lies north of the equator. The word *micro* means "little" and comes from the Greek word *mikros*. This geographic area contains more than three thousand different islands. The best known are the Mariana Islands, the Marshalls, Kiribati, and the Federated States of Micronesia.

The third major Pacific Island group is Polynesia—*poly* meaning "many" in Greek. This area is often defined as a triangle drawn from the islands of Hawaii in the north, Easter Island in the southeast, and New Zealand in the southwest. Within the triangle are the islands of French Polynesia, Tonga, Samoa, and the Cook Islands. The islands not included in these groupings are those that make up the Philippines and Indonesia, which are geographically a part of Asia, not the Pacific.

These divisions, however, are strictly geographic in nature, for there are no clear-cut cultural boundaries between the different societies who live there. Many island cultures, for instance, are composite societies, made up of representatives from several different backgrounds. This is due primarily to the large amount of crossover that has occurred among the various peoples of the Pacific.

The Pacific Islanders

While each island group has had a distinct history and a unique experience, they do share a few common historical elements. According to historian David Howarth, "[The islands] had been left entirely alone since mankind first came to live in them, and [the indigenous people] had all the needs of human life and comfort. . . . Unthreatened, they created a society and a religion on the basis that there

was plenty of everything for everyone. . . . They were perfectly content with what they had."[2]

Beginning in the sixteenth century, after hundreds of years of relative isolation, the indigenous people of the Pacific were quite suddenly confronted by another race of people they did not know existed. During the years that followed the arrival in the islands of Europeans, nearly all of the islanders saw the development of plantation agriculture and the use of their people as workers and slaves. Eventually coming

A native of New Guinea. Pacific Islanders were isolated until European explorers arrived in the 1500s.

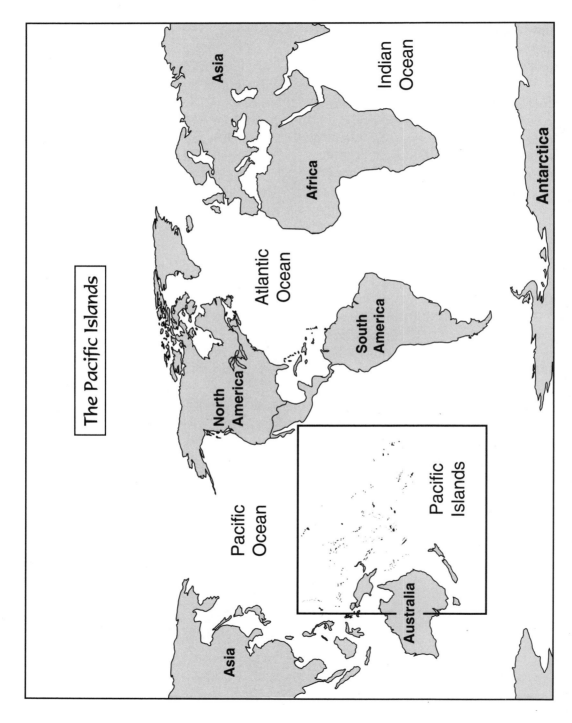

The Pacific Islands

Asia

Indian
Ocean

Africa

Antarctica

Atlantic
Ocean

South
America

North
America

Pacific
Ocean

Pacific
Islands

Asia

Australia

under the control of foreign governments, the islanders saw many of their customs and traditions repressed and destroyed by outside forces.

Since the 1950s most Pacific Island countries have gained some form of independence. At the same time, however, many indigenous peoples become minority populations in their own homeland. Moreover, they often face problems stemming from unemployment, racism, and alcoholism that were unknown to their ancestors.

Life has changed significantly for the indigenous peoples of the Pacific since their early beginnings. In recent years, however, a cultural renaissance has occurred throughout the region. Despite the hardships of the past and present, their traditional heritage and culture are once again thriving in the Pacific.

Chapter 1

The Great Migration

"The Pacific region," according to historian Robert C. Kiste, "was the last major world area to be occupied by human beings. . . . It [also] became the last major area of the world to be probed by representatives of the western world, . . . to experience colonization at the hands of the Western powers and . . . to achieve independence and/or self government."[3]

The settlement of the Pacific, according to historians, occurred in several broad phases. During the first, nearly fifty thou-

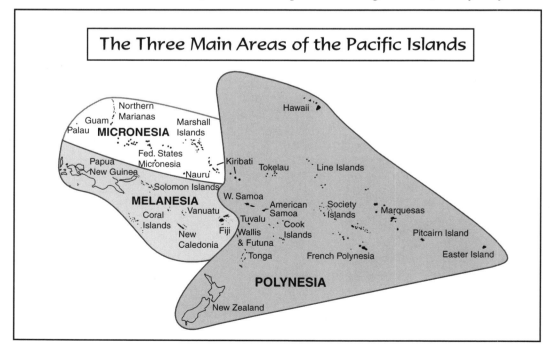

The Three Main Areas of the Pacific Islands

Northern Marianas
Hawaii
Guam
Palau **MICRONESIA**
Marshall Islands
Fed. States Micronesia
Papua New Guinea
Kiribati
Tokelau
Line Islands
Nauru
Solomon Islands
W. Samoa
MELANESIA
American Samoa
Society Islands
Marquesas
Vanuatu
Coral Islands
Tuvalu
Cook Islands
New Caledonia
Fiji
Wallis & Futuna
Pitcairn Island
French Polynesia
Easter Island
Tonga
POLYNESIA
New Zealand

sand years ago, Australia and New Guinea were discovered and settled by explorers from Southeast Asia. While the newcomers would become the Aborigines in Australia, in New Guinea they became the Papuans, one of the world's earliest fisherpeople and agriculturists. No further extended exploration occurred until around 3000 B.C., a year that marks the second phase of exploration and settlement and the discovery of the islands of Fiji, Tonga, and Samoa by a new wave of Asian seafarers.

Thor Heyerdahl

Thor Heyerdahl, who died in 2002 at the age of eighty-seven, was a best-selling Norwegian writer, explorer, and scholar. While working on his Ph.D. in the 1940s, Heyerdahl became convinced that the first Pacific Island inhabitants came not from Asia and Indonesia but from South America.

Heyerdahl decided to test his theory. In 1947 he and five shipmates built a balsa raft employing techniques that had been utilized by the Incas, an advanced and ancient civilization from Peru in South America. Heyerdahl and his crew set out for Polynesia in a thirty-five-foot raft that they christened the *Kon-Tiki*. After over one hundred days at sea they landed on a small uninhabited island in Polynesia. Heyerdahl recorded the story of his voyage in the book *Kon-Tiki*, which became an international best-seller.

Heyerdahl based his beliefs on the similarity of Easter Island statues to ancient Inca art and also on a few references that he found in ancient writings describing early Inca voyages. While his books were wildly popular, other historians have not supported Heyerdahl's findings and conclusions. In the late twentieth century his theo-

Thor Heyerdahl admires a shark he caught at sea aboard his raft, the Kon-Tiki, *in 1947.*

ries were completely disproved. Scientists now theorize that it was the Polynesians who visited South America—and not the other way around.

Nearly a thousand years would pass before the next major wave of migration occurred. From the already inhabited islands of the Pacific, great waves of indigenous explorers and settlers sailed east looking for new homelands. This phase is often referred to as the "Great Migration." It would result in the settlement of island after island in the area of the Pacific known as Polynesia. "With the settlement of New Zealand in 1200 A.D.," writes historian Goran Burenhult, "the expansion of prehistoric habitation in the Pacific came to an end."[4]

Asian Origins

Although the question of where the indigenous people of the Pacific originated stumped archaeologists and historians for years, it is now almost universally agreed that they came from Southeast Asia. A few scholars, including the late Norwegian writer and explorer Thor Heyerdahl, have argued that the people of the Pacific actually originated in South America. This supposition has been seriously challenged by recent DNA studies. Journalist Simon Robinson, writing in 1998, elaborates: "Over the past decade, scientists have found genetic links between Polynesians and a people who lived in what is now eastern China and Taiwan around five thousand years ago."[5]

Recent scholarship and archaeology have also revealed the existence of a culture known as Lapita that arose in Southeast

A Melanesian pottery maker carefully shapes the lip of a vase. Both functional and artistic, this craft has been refined and passed down for generations.

Asia more than three thousand years ago. Pottery samples that have been discovered in Southeast Asia and also on various Pacific Islands point to a common heritage. This pottery is characterized by intricate geometric designs added to the clay prior to firing. According to Burenhult, "Remains of Lapita people in Fiji and other islands reveal a tall, slender people who bear some similarities to . . . modern Polynesians."[6]

Another indication of Asian origin lies in the similarities between the Asians and

16

the Pacific Islanders and their cultures. According to the editors of Time-Life Books, "It [is] . . . apparent that similar cultures, as expressed in the form of their houses, beliefs, funeral customs and agricultural practices existed for some time across mainland Indochina . . . New Guinea and the islands of Micronesia and Polynesia."[7]

This common ancestry is also evident in the similarity of appearances and languages and the commonality of their domestic animals and plants. All of the islanders, for instance, speak some form of the Austronesian language group that originated in Southeast Asia. The indigenous people of the Pacific Islands speak over 1,200 of the world's 3,000 languages, with nearly 700 of them spoken on Papua, New Guinea alone. While island dialects vary greatly from place to place, there are many similarities in the different languages.

The First Phase of Pacific Settlement

New Guinea, the second largest island in the world (only Greenland is bigger), was the first island in the Pacific, along with the continent of Australia, to be settled by migrating Asians. Once they arrived in New Guinea the people quickly adapted to their new homeland by becoming expert fishermen. Indeed, great fishermen were highly honored throughout the Pacific. On many islands, after a fisherman died, family members carved fishhooks from his bones. It was believed that his bones held power and good luck.

Early Fishing Techniques

In the early days especially, fishing off New Guinea was generally easy because of the shallow waters of the coral reefs and the abundance of fish. According to Burenhult, "Prehistoric fishermen in the Pacific used a quite bewildering variety of techniques, including basket fish traps, kite fishing, poisoning techniques, . . . fishhooks, nets, spears, and bows and arrows."[8]

Basket traps were used to catch marine eels and many different types of fish. The traps were made from thorny vines and coconut or other plant fiber. Bait was fastened inside a cone-shaped basket and then lowered on a line into the shallow water. When a fish came after the bait, it became trapped on the thorns and was easily captured by the fisherman.

One of the most unique fishing methods was a technique called kite fishing. Kite fishermen used spider webs to create a sticky trap for the fish. The webs were attached to the tail of a kite, which was made from leaves or vines. Paddling just offshore, fishermen in canoes flew their kites low over the water, where the motion of the tail attracted large quantities of fish. Their teeth were quickly caught in the sticky substance on the line, enabling the fisherman to pull them easily into the canoe.

Occasionally a mild poison called rotenone was used to catch fish. This substance, which comes from the root of the derris vine, prevents fish from breathing. A small amount of the poison poured into the water of a lake or stream would cause the fish to stop breathing and float to the surface where they were hauled in by nets.

The people on other Pacific Islands quickly adopted many of the Papuans' techniques, while also adding a few new ones of their own. On the Melanesian island of Fiji, for instance, the villagers jumped into freshwater lakes and stirred up the water with their hands. This activity caused the fish to leap out of the water where they were easily caught in nets made of vines. Other Melanesian fishermen who lived along coral reefs used a similar technique. An entire village formed a large circle on the reef during high tide. Holding a loop made of leaves and vines, the natives sang and beat the water as they began to close the circle, trapping the fish within their human enclosure.

Early Shipbuilders

The people who settled in New Guinea were not only expert fishers but also shipbuilders who developed a type of canoe known as a *lakatoi*. The men who built and sailed these vessels were selected with great care. The crew was guided by a "big leader," or *baditauna*, and the entire group had to follow a very strict ceremonial process. During the building these men could not talk to their wives, nor could they eat certain foods or cut their hair.

A kite fisherman deploys his kite slightly above the water in hopes of catching a fish in his sticky trap.

Four large logs were hollowed out and lashed together with plant vines to form a hull. At that point a shaman or medicine man was called upon to bless the vessel with "magic smoke" from burning incense. Decking was then added along with a lean-to type shelter that would house the crew and cargo. The sailors' wives sewed sails by braiding palm fronds together and, on the top of each wooden mast, the men attached a totem, the symbol of their clan.

Construction took around a month to complete. Food was stored aboard and a great ceremonial feast was held just prior to departure. Until their husbands returned from the voyage, the women were required to keep a hearth fire burning. The natives believed that if this fire went out the men would face disaster and the voyage would end tragically. A huge feast was also held when the sailors returned.

These sailing voyages, or *huri*, were attempted only at the times of year when the prevailing winds were blowing in a favorable direction. The trips, which were for purposes of trade, could span hundreds of miles and take anywhere from three to four months to complete. The last *huri* in New Guinea occurred in 1940.

Early Farmers

Gradually, over a period of thousands of years, the original Papuans moved inland to become one of the world's first agricultural peoples. Some of the villagers grew large vegetable gardens that were drained by man-made ditches as many as nine

A *Papuan farmer hand cultivates his land to improve crop yields.*

thousand years ago. They were successful in cultivating bananas, yams, sugarcane, peanuts, and many other crops. The abundance of available food enabled the new populations to thrive and grow.

The people of the various islands in the Pacific took their agricultural practices very seriously. With their very lives depending on the production of crops, every facet of farming took on a near-religious significance. Special ceremonies and rituals were held at each stage of the agriculture process—planting, maturation, and harvest. Rules were also developed that denoted strict times of year for cultivation.

The Last Phase of Settlement

By around 500 B.C. the Melanesian peoples of New Guinea and Fiji, along with the early Polynesians of Tonga and Samoa, had formed villages and settled down. Around the same time, a new wave of immigrants from Asia also flooded the Pacific region, causing overpopulation problems on many of the smaller islands. Due to limited land, food, and other natural resources, thousands of people were faced with starvation. As a result, vast numbers of people began looking elsewhere for land to colonize. Setting forth from Hawaiki, an island believed to be the homeland of many Polynesian people, and other sites, they turned north and east to the islands of Micronesia and Polynesia.

Another factor that may have contributed to this final migration was the almost constant warfare that occurred between rival chiefs and tribes. It is also conceivable that the people simply became restless and, responding to a need for adventure, set out and looked for new places to explore.

The Great Migration

Polynesian historian David Kawaharada characterizes the migration to Hawaii and other parts of the Pacific as "one of the most remarkable achievements of humanity. . . . The migration began before the birth of Christ. While the Europeans were [still] sailing close to the coastlines of continents . . . voyagers from Fiji, Tonga, and Samoa began to settle the islands [of the Pacific]."[9]

The achievements of these prehistoric navigators and explorers are nothing short of astonishing when one considers the immense body of water they crossed. Their skills were sufficient to find islands sometimes less than a mile in diameter on which the highest landmark was a tall tree. Not only could they find the new islands in the first place, but they also were able to unerringly return to them without difficulty. According to National Geographic writers Frans Lanting and Christine K. Eckstrom, their "skills [were] unsurpassed by any other people on earth."[10]

Those who settled the Pacific Islands used a fairly deliberate system of exploration. Kawaharada writes: "[This system] involved waiting for a reversal in wind direction and sailing in that direction which is normally upwind (eastward in the Pacific) for as far as it was safe to go given the supplies that were carried on the canoe. The return home (westward) would be made when the wind shifted back to its normal . . . direction."[11]

These early explorers were able to sail immense distances by reading the stars at night and the ocean waves during daylight hours. They could estimate their canoe's position by mentally calculating time, speed, and distance; all without the use of modern navigational equipment. They were able to predict the presence of land by observing changes in the patterns of waves, certain cloud formations, the flight paths of land-dwelling birds, and the presence of certain plants in the water.

Kupe

The Maori of New Zealand believe that an ancient and brilliant explorer named Kupe was the first to discover their homeland. More than one thousand years ago, according to native belief, Kupe set sail from Hawaiki, the Polynesian homeland. This island, although the name is quite similar, was not Hawaii but rather an island in the Marquesas, which is now part of French Polynesia. Hawaiki would also serve as the home base for various other Polynesian explorers and settlers.

With his family and friends Kupe crossed the Pacific in canoes in search of new lands. Maori legends report that after a long and difficult journey Kupe's wife suddenly saw what she thought was a cloud in the distance. In actuality, it was the island of New Zealand which Kupe would later name *Aotearoa*—the "land of the long white cloud." After exploring this new land Kupe returned to Hawaiki with tales of abundant land and natural riches. Despite the appeal of this distant land, no further efforts were made to colonize the new island until centuries later when overpopulation and a shortage of food finally drove the people to send settlers to the land Kupe had discovered.

According to Maori legends, ten great canoes set forth from Hawaiki. Families brought dogs and various agricultural plants with them and landed at ten different sites in New Zealand. Today the indigenous people say that every Maori can trace his or her ancestry back to one of the families on the ten canoes.

In addition, these navigators made simple, yet accurate, instruments to aid them in their return to previously discovered land. According to the editors of Reader's Digest Books, "for often used routes, [they] constructed charts using sticks bound together to illustrate routes and currents, and small shells and stones to indicate islands."[12]

The dangers involved in such voyages were immense. The sailors were constantly exposed to wind, rain, and sun and had little covering or clothing for protection. Starvation was a constant danger because of limited food and water supplies.

There was also the possibility of the relatively small and overcrowded vessels swamping or capsizing in the heavy seas of the Pacific. Sails made of nothing but natural fiber could easily be torn, while unseen reefs and rocks posed a threat to wooden canoe hulls. That they survived and were able to successfully colonize the Pacific was and is a testament to their courage and skill.

Carrying with them their common family of languages and their cultural traditions and ways of life, these prehistoric seafarers ranged halfway around the world. By the time the Europeans entered

Two Tahitian seafarers set out on their sturdy double-hulled canoe carrying a heavy load to a nearby island.

the Pacific around A.D. 1520, the expansion, migration, and colonization had largely ceased. By that time, according to Burenhult, "on most of the islands, the people had given up long-distance voyaging and were concentrating on internal matters."[13]

Polynesian Shipbuilding

The settlement of the numerous and remote Pacific Islands depended on the development of a vessel that was capable of long ocean voyages. Early Polynesian seafarers found their answer in two different vessels—the outrigger canoe and the double-hulled canoe.

The double-hulled canoe, resembling a present-day catamaran, was the vessel most commonly used for these long ocean voyages. The hulls were dug out from tree trunks with stone tools and then joined together by a platform on which a mast was erected. Plant fiber, usually coconut palm, was used to "sew" everything together, while cracks and seams were sealed with a mixture of sap and plant fiber to prevent leakage. A simple shelter made of coconut fronds or pandanus leaves was provided for the families and also for storage of food and water supplies. The double-hulled canoe had tremendous stability and was able to safely carry large groups of people along with all their belongings and the items they would need for survival at sea.

Outrigger canoes were also used by many Polynesian cultures. These vessels had a single hull but were given stability by the addition of outrigger floats that were attached to one or both sides. Sails were added to both types of canoe. These were made of plant matting, usually from the salt and water-resistant leaves of the pandanus tree, an Asian tree noted for its long and narrow leaves that can easily be sewn together. The canoes were sailed when there was wind and paddled when there was not. Both types of vessels were seaworthy enough to make ocean voyages of over two thousand miles.

The early explorers of the Pacific also carried with them various plants such as banana, coconut, taro, sago, and paper mulberry. These were transplanted in each new land they discovered. Along with seeds and plants the settlers also brought with them domesticated livestock, mainly in the form of pigs and chickens. These plants and animals quickly flourished in their new tropical climates.

As the indigenous people began to adapt to life in new and interesting places, a rich way of life developed that would sustain them for another thousand years.

Chapter 2

Everyday Life in the Pacific

Most of the islands in the Pacific are tropical in nature, with high humidity, frequent rain, and warm daily temperatures averaging between sixty-eight and eighty-one degrees Fahrenheit. As journalist Bill Strubbe states, the islands are a "tropical dream come true; rustling palm trees, fringing the shimmering white sands, idyllic lagoons"[14] all create an image of breathtaking beauty.

Today, tourists who relish white sandy beaches and warm tropical waters find abundant vacation spots on the islands of the Pacific.

Surfing

Riding the waves has been a popular pastime throughout the ages on the islands of the Pacific. It was in Hawaii, however, that the sport of surfing was perfected. In early Hawaii the ruling classes allowed the workers to relax and put down their tools during a special yearly festival called *makahiki*. During this time of year the young men swam, boxed, threw spears in competition, and surfed.

Pictures of surfing (the sport is called *he'e nalu* in Hawaii) were left in rock drawings called petroglyphs that have been discovered throughout the islands. These pictures depict the proficiency and talent of early Polynesians who used wooden boards up to sixteen feet in length to ride the waves. In fact, many European explorers of the sixteenth and seventeenth centuries reported their astonishment at being greeted with offshore contingents of nearly naked men riding these long surfboards. While most paddled out lying flat on the boards, others were standing up, giving the appearance of seeming to walk on the water.

A Hawaiian is also credited with being the "father" of modern surfing. Duke Kahanamoku (1890–1968) is a Hawaiian hero. He is credited with introducing surfing to Australia and California, developing the rules for modern surfing contests, and pioneering the development of windsurfing, which uses a sail to give extra power to the surfboard. Kahanamoku was also a competitive swimmer and won gold and silver medals in the 1912 and 1920 Olympics.

A surfer braves the face of a massive wave off the island of Hawaii.

The thatched roof of a Pacific island hut is set in place over the hut's hardwood frame (left). The tightly woven roof prevents rain from seeping through (above).

As the various indigenous people of the Pacific settled in these comfortable new homelands, a number of very diverse cultures developed. One of the most important factors that determined a people's way of life was the actual physical environment of the island on which they settled.

Features of the Pacific Islands

There are several kinds of islands in the Pacific. High islands, which are volcanic in origin, tend to be hilly and have soils well suited to farming. Low islands, on the other hand, are usually formed by the buildup of coral. Over millions of years

coral reefs, composed of the skeletons of tiny sea animals, become attached to a core of rock and gradually rise above the ocean's surface. These islands are less suited to farming, but are rich in fish and other marine life.

A small number of Pacific Islands, including New Zealand, New Guinea, and Fiji, were once part of a huge landmass that included Asia and Australia. These islands are unique in the Pacific in that they have large rivers, fertile soil, and a good freshwater supply. Life was much more varied on these few islands.

Despite the varied physical environments of the islands, the indigenous people shared many similarities in their ways of life. For example, most of them were accomplished boatbuilders who used canoes for fishing, trade, and travel. In addition, subsistence farming, or the growing of plants and vegetables for personal and community use, was common throughout the Pacific. The people all used simple tools made out of bone, shell, and stone and raised animals that had originally been imported to the islands.

Island Homes

As the various indigenous people of the Pacific colonized and settled on their new island homes, one of their most immediate needs was finding shelter. Toward that end, the natives built many different kinds of homes depending on climate, the amount of rain received, and the terrain in which they lived.

On some of the more mountainous islands, the natives chose to live in caves. On islands where large rock quarries were available, people built stone houses. So expertly were these dwellings constructed that many were airtight despite the lack of mortar. The Rapa Nui people of Easter Island, for instance, built unusual canoe-shaped stone houses that were reserved for priests or other men of nobility and high ranking.

Most Pacific Islanders, however, lived in one-room thatched huts, usually rectangular in shape. Made of palm leaves or bamboo, these homes were easy and quick to build and, despite needing frequent upkeep and maintenance, could last up to

twenty years. They also were able to withstand the force of typhoon winds while keeping the occupants dry and safe.

The frames of these thatched huts generally were made from hardwood and then enclosed with tightly woven bamboo or other plant material to form walls. Thatched palm leaves were fastened across the top to form a roof in which a small vent was cut so that smoke from the hearth fire could escape. The floors were usually made of sand or dirt, while a curtain made of plant material usually separated the sleeping area from the rest of the house. The islanders used little to no furniture, preferring instead to sleep on some kind of mattress made from plant materials. Many of these thatched homes were built on stilts, especially when located near the ocean or along rivers.

The Hewa people of Papua, New Guinea lived in tree houses. Journalist Edward Marriott spent several months in that country and reports: "They build a platform first, then weave banana leaves through the branches to make a roof. They live very high up, perhaps a hundred feet."[15] Other natives of New Guinea built large rectangular homes over a hundred feet long called *yews*. The *yews* resembled apartment houses with each family group having its own dwelling.

Island Dress

The indigenous people of the Pacific wore little if any clothing because of the warm tropical climate. If men wore anything it was usually a simple loincloth made of some natural plant material. Women tended to go topless and wore a traditional grass skirt or apron over the lower half of their bodies. During ceremonial dances and other rituals both sexes wore skirts and decorative accessories.

Many of the early Polynesian colonists brought along trees called paper mulberry to plant in their new homelands. This Asian tree produces a bark that can be pounded into thin pieces and then used as a kind of cloth. After soaking in sea water, the bark was beaten with wooden or stone mallets until it was paper thin. Called *tapa* in parts

A tapa *clothmaker displays his design.* Tapa *is made by beating or pounding the bark of a paper mulberry tree.*

of Polynesia and *masi* in parts of Melanesia, the cloth made from this tree was used widely for clothing throughout the Pacific.

This bark was often dyed a rust color from red clay and black color made from the bark of mangrove trees. Another method of dyeing the cloth was to bury it in mud—a process that caused a black stain.

The names for traditional garments differed from island to island but in appearance the clothing was much the same. In Samoa, for instance, women wore a garment called a *lava lava*, a rather simple body wrap. When they danced they wore a grass skirt called a *siva*. In Fiji the traditional garment worn by both sexes was the *sulu*, a wraparound skirt made of bark cloth. The *sulu*, when worn by women, came down to the ankles, while the men's stopped at mid-calf. A shorter *sulu* was part of the Fijian military uniform. And in Papua New Guinea, men wore traditional mid-calf wraparound skirts known as *lap lap*.

Clothing Accessories

Hats were particularly popular on many Pacific Islands. On the Cook Islands, for instance, *rito* hats are still worn by women to church every Sunday. These hats are made from coconut palm fiber and are considered important possessions. Similar to panama hats, they are usually adorned with hatbands made of small shells.

String bags called *bilums* were (and still are) carried by Papua New Guinea natives. Made of natural plant materials, the bags are used to carry everything from produce to firewood. In addition, many of the women use the bags to carry pigs to market and also for carrying their infant children.

Islanders in the Pacific frequently wore necklaces made of shark's teeth, shells, or even the teeth of dead relatives. Most people wore some form of jewelry and many had elaborate bone ornaments inserted in their nasal septums along with elaborate ear decorations. Women used the seed of the lipstick plant to stain and paint their faces. Various natural dyes were also used to paint complex facial designs during ritual ceremonies and festivals.

Adorned with feathers, dyes, and bones, a "wig man" of New Guinea prepares for a ritual ceremony.

Many islanders also wore enormous headdresses that were adorned with beautiful feathers and shells. The Huli villagers of Tari in Papua New Guinea, for instance, were often called the "wig men." They were noted for their huge wigs made out of human hair, some of which had come from ancestors who, long before their deaths, had cut off and saved long tresses of their hair. The wigs were usually adorned with animal furs, flowers, grasses, and feathers.

Food on the Islands

The Asian people who settled the Pacific Islands brought most of their own food with them when they migrated. Various plants and seeds were planted upon arrival and formed the nucleus of their diet. In addition, they made use of whatever native plant and animal species that existed on the various islands.

One of the most important foods was a starchy material made from the sago palm tree. To prepare sago for eating, the bark was stripped from the tree to expose the inner fibrous pith. Women, using a blunt club, hammered the pith until it was the consistency of sawdust. The pith was then soaked and kneaded like bread dough and forced through a woven sieve that separated the sago flour from the woody pith. After draining off any excess water, the sago flour was wrapped in leaves, dried, and then made into hard cakes, which were baked in pits called ground ovens or cooked over open fires.

In many parts of the Pacific, yams (which are similar to sweet potatoes) were grown to large sizes and held special symbolic meaning. In Papua New Guinea, for instance, it was widely believed that eating yams would result in increased strength and virility. Coconuts provided both milk and coconut meat, while wild plants such

Ground Ovens

The indigenous people of the Pacific Islands made wide use of ground ovens for the purposes of cooking. Although they went by various names—*umu* on Easter Island, *hangi* by the Maori of New Zealand—the ovens were quite similar in construction and use.

Ground ovens are simply pits that are dug into the earth and then used to cook meats and vegetables. Building such an oven was usually a group or village event. After digging a hole around three feet deep the people built a wood fire inside the pit. They added stones which were heated up until the original wood burned down to ashes. After the flames died out a layer of fern fronds or other leaves was added; food was wrapped in more leaves and then placed in the oven, followed by another layer of grass or plant material. Water was sprinkled over everything and the pit was closed using either earth or special mats made out of flax.

The meat and vegetables cooked slowly for several hours. This same procedure is still used on many of the Pacific Islands today. In Hawaii the resulting feast is called a luau.

Polynesian men tend to a ground oven at a luau in Hawaii.

Before a crocodile capture, Papuans perform a crocodile dance ritual to ensure a safe and successful hunt.

as spinach were also an important part of the islanders' diets.

Crocodile meat was a mainstay in the diet of many natives of Papua New Guinea. The fearsome reptile is still hunted today by a capture method that is quite startling to outsiders. The men enter the murky water barefoot and begin to walk all around the riverbed until someone steps on a submerged crocodile. The animal, enraged from the contact, leaps up to grab the hunter, who then grabs the creature around its jaws and wrestles or spears it. Pigs and chickens, descended from stock brought by the early settlers, pro-

vided the main source of meat in many other parts of the Pacific, while islanders who lived near the sea relied on fishing as their primary food source.

In general Pacific Islanders ate with their hands. Even today, very few eat with a knife or fork, especially in small villages where meals are still eaten on the floor. Most ate outside. The practice of eating indoors in the same house where people slept was forbidden or taboo. Many natives believed that if the food was brought inside a building, the structure would have to be burned down. In Melanesia cooking was also done in a building separate from the sleeping quarters.

Native Drinks

Water and coconut milk were the main drinks in most areas of the Pacific. In Fiji, however, the adults drank kava. During a visit to Fiji, *National Geographic* journalist Roger Vaughan had the opportunity to taste this national beverage. He wrote: "Kava is a brown, non-alcoholic drink made of water and the crushed roots of a pepper plant and drunk from a coconut cup called a *bilo*. It has a mild anesthetic effect, gently numbing lips, mouth and mind. It tastes like a combination of muddy river water and yesterday's tea."[16]

Kava is made from the pepper plant *piper methysticum* and, in the past, was primarily drunk during traditional ceremonies that celebrated births, deaths, marriages, and other important events. This ceremony, attended only by men, was called a *yaqona* and was held in the community meeting or spirit house. During this ritual the only utensils used were of ancient design, as prescribed by tradition.

The participants sat in a circle on a large woven mat while the guest of honor sat directly in front of the kava bowl, or *tanoa*. A special server was responsible for making the drink. The *tanoa* was filled with water and the kava leaves, wrapped in a cloth, was added until the water turned brown. The server filled a *bilo* with the mixture and handed it to the guest of honor who clapped once and drank down the entire contents in one swallow and then clapped three more times. The cup was refilled and passed to each man, who repeated the same ritual, until all had the opportunity to drink. No one spoke during the entire ceremony.

The kava ritual is still performed in many parts of Melanesia today. Once picked and prepared by special individuals, the drink is now available in an instant powdered form and also comes in "kava bars." Many businesses keep bowls of kava for their employees to drink during their lunch hours and break periods.

The indigenous people of the Micronesian island of Pohnpei have a similar drink called *sakua*. According to the editors of National Geographic Books, "*Sakua* is a slimy narcotic drink essential to every ritual and formal occasion. It is made from pepper plant roots pounded to shreds on a rock with a large flat surface. Water is poured over the pulp, and the mixture is strained through a wrapping of hibiscus bark strips and wrung into a coconut shell."[17]

Many Melanesians also chew a mild stimulant called betel. According to traditional belief and experience, betel nut helps relieve tiredness and hunger. It also causes the teeth to become black while staining the gums and lips a bright red or black.

Traditional Dance

Dance was and is a cherished and sacred part of life throughout the Pacific. The dances told stories and were performed by well-trained individuals, many of whom spent their entire lives studying and practicing the art. According to the *Lonely Planet's Guide* "Among the Kanaks [of New Caledonia] dance has developed into a high art form. The traditional *pilou* dance tells the stories of births, marriages, cyclones or preparations for battle."[18]

Many dances were actually used to teach history to the younger generations. This was particularly true on the island of Fiji where a musical tradition called the *meke* was performed. Combining song, dance, and theater, the meke centered around the reenacting of legends and stories from Fijian history.

In New Guinea most dances were performed during special celebrations called *sing-sings*. During these enactments of historical events, costumed men and women took on roles representing birds, trees, animals, and spirits. These dances were held to celebrate a variety of events ranging from initiation rites to marriage.

The best known of any traditional dance is probably the hula of Hawaii. According to writer Moana Tregaskis, "The hula originated, legend says, when the volcano goddess Pele commanded her younger sister Laka to dance."[19] Shortly after the Hawaiian Islands were settled various schools of hula were formed to honor

Laka, while numerous temples were dedicated in her honor. Native dancers lived in the temples and spent hundreds of hours in strenuous training programs. According to Tregaskis, "[hula] represented the heart of the people . . . to the Hawaiians [it] celebrates life."[20]

In New Zealand, Maori men performed a war dance called the *laka* before going

An islander wrings a pepper plant through hibiscus fibers while another catches the freshly squeezed sakua *in a coconut shell.*

into battle. Carrying spears and clubs, the dancers chanted while making faces and sticking out their tongues. The women in Maori society performed a *poi*, or ball dance, that consisted of graceful movements while twirling balls made of fiber.

Island Artisans

Artisans were highly respected and revered among the various indigenous societies of the Pacific. According to the editors of National Geographic Books, "when a powerful chief wanted an object of great social and spiritual significance such as a sacred canoe . . . an expert was engaged to produce it."[21]

The Maori of New Zealand, for instance, were superb stone carvers. One tribe, the Ngati Porou, believed that carving was a gift handed down by the gods. According to their legends, writes *National Geographic* journalist Douglas Newton, "Carving was unknown among men until the sea god Tangaroa kidnapped the son of the mythical hero Rua. While rescuing the boy, Rua found the god's richly adorned house and, before burning it, stole carvings to copy for his own home."[22]

Greenstone, another name for jade in parts of the Pacific, was a prized possession among several indigenous groups. Highly trained specialists carved greenstone figures that were worn as pendants. Because of its hardness, greenstone was also used for making tools such as adzes and chisels.

Fijian women perform a meke *to enlighten others about their cultural heritage.*

A little girl sits wearing a handmade grass skirt. One day she will be taught to weave rugs, grass skirts, and other clothes made out of leaves.

Weaving was a very special art form in parts of Polynesia. Using bark, grass, and leaves, women created rugs, grass skirts, and other clothing. Their greatest achievement, however, was the weaving of floor mats made from high quality pandanus. The brown pandanus bark and leaves were soaked in water, baked, and then scraped until they were thin and of a near golden whiteness. When this preparatory process was complete, the weaver was left with strands only one-sixteenth of an inch in width. The weaving of a three-by-four-foot mat could take as long as two years to complete.

Whether in their intricate weaving or beautiful dances, the indigenous people of the Pacific left behind a rich heritage and legacy that continues to astound and amaze modern historians and visitors.

Chapter 3

Island Communities and Families

The structure of society varied greatly from one Pacific Island to another. As a general rule, Polynesian societies were stratified, or separated into several social classes. There was always a wide gap between those at the top—the nobility—and the remainder of the people who were commoners. Unlike the Polynesians, who were chiefs because of birthright, the Melanesian tribal leaders attained their positions through hard work and brave deeds. On the islands of Micronesia, authority resided in elderly men or chiefs who formed a council of chiefs and retained special privileges as was common on Polynesian islands.

Polynesian Chiefs

Polynesian chiefs had near total authority over their people, commanding respect and deference. According to a Polynesian website, "Allegiance to chiefs was a fundamental part of Polynesian culture."[23] Special spiritual power called *mana* attributed to the chiefs who exercised both political and economic leadership and were often believed to be descendants of the gods.

While heads of families usually handled day-to-day matters, chiefs were responsible for the problems and decisions that involved the entire village or tribe. One of the most important responsibilities of a chief was to organize, sponsor, and pay for feasts and festivals. In fact, a man was often judged by his willingness to throw big parties and provide gifts for others.

Social structure on the islands of Hawaii was stratified into four classes: the *alii* were a group of chiefs and nobles; the *kahuna* were priests and educated men; the *makaainana* were hardworking commoners; and the *kauwa* were outcasts. The *kauwa* lived in segregated areas and were frequently used as human sacrifices.

The division of Polynesian society into classes was strictly enforced through a taboo system that controlled daily life. Taboos, called *kapu* in Hawaii, were sanctions or rules that governed all contact between royalty and the common people.

In Maori society on New Zealand, for instance, a chief's body was considered sacred from the time he was born and could not be touched by ordinary people. In many societies commoners were required to fall prostrate on the ground when a member of the nobility passed by. An ordinary person who so much as stepped on the shadow of a chief faced immediate death.

Melanesia and Male Dominated Society

According to historian Robert C. Kiste, "Nowhere in . . . [the Pacific] are the differences between the sexes as marked as in Melanesia."[24] Women commonly performed heavy work, had their own separate houses and gardens, and were forbidden to eat many of the foods eaten by men. In Fiji, women were treated with such little respect that when a man died, his wife was frequently strangled so she could accompany him on his journey into the afterlife.

Throughout the Melanesian islands there was a strict division of labor. Men built houses, hunted, fought, and supervised and protected their families. Women, on the other hand, were responsible for everything else, including planting gardens, cooking, carrying firewood, cleaning, tending the family's pigs, raising children, and making clothes. Very young children usually lived with their mother or other female relative,

but boys moved into their father's home when they were around six or seven.

Women were forbidden to enter community or spirit houses. This was due, in part, to men's fear that the power inherent in women, if allowed to be present everywhere, could weaken men's physical strength and sexual potency. For that reason, women were kept strictly segregated during menstruation and after childbirth.

This decorated Papuan chief is responsible for making important decisions, solving problems, and throwing lavish parties for the people of his tribe.

Warfare

Warfare was a universal and constant fact of life for Pacific Island societies. In most places every adult male was a warrior who was highly skilled in combat with traditional clubs, spears, and other weapons. Chiefs were generally responsible for leadership during tribal warfare.

In addition to fights for land and power, conflicts frequently broke out for the purpose of revenge. According to the editors of Reader's Digest Books, "Insult or injury to one person would be seen as an insult to his whole tribe and vengeance would be sought, usually by means of a military raid."[25] The neighboring village would then feel obliged to retaliate, causing the killing to go on and on.

Constant warfare led many of the early islanders to build fortified villages as a defense against future enemy attacks. Around A.D. 1000, for instance, when a group of Polynesians invaded Fiji, the Fijians fled into an area protected by enormous ring-ditch fortifications. On the islands of New Zealand, the Maori built forts called *pa*, which were surrounded by various earthworks. These were usually built to take full advantage of any landscape that helped with defense, such as rivers, mountains, or large rocks.

Cannibalism and Head-Hunting

Cannibalism was nearly universal among the Pacific Islanders and played an important role in their cultures for nearly twenty-five hundred years. The practice

A New Guinea warrior armed with a bow and arrow. All male Pacific Islanders are taught at a young age to be fearless fighters.

was largely stopped after the arrival of European missionaries in the nineteenth century, but some isolated tribes in Papua New Guinea continued to eat human flesh well into the twentieth century. Cannibalism was so widespread on the islands of Fiji, in fact, that early European explorers called Fiji the "Cannibal Isles."

The worst fate that could befall a warrior was to be eaten by the enemy. Melanesians, in particular, believed that such an end destroyed an individual's soul and spirit. Writer Tony Wheeler reports, "Eating an enemy was a way not only to deliver the ultimate insult but also to take on the enemy's life force, mana, or power."[26]

During wartime many bodies were eaten raw right on the battlefield. Prisoners were often brought back to the village where some were killed and given in sacrifice to the gods. One of the most horrifying practices was to make victims watch different parts of their own bodies being eaten; even worse was forcing them to eat these parts themselves.

Warriors usually kept the victim's head after removing the lower jaw. The jawbone was frequently worn as a necklace, a sym-

bolic emblem of a warrior's proficiency in battle. In the late eighteenth century, market forces stimulated the practice of headhunting in the Pacific. Wheeler reports that in New Zealand, European sailors supposedly "created such a demand for preserved heads that Maori chiefs started chopping off their slaves' heads to order."[27]

The Polynesian Concept of Family

Despite the presence of widespread violence between tribes, most indigenous groups lived in harmony within their own communities, usually made up of extended

Extended families are common in the Pacific Islands. Children are shared between households and frequently call multiple people their parents.

family members. The concept of extended family played a particularly significant role in Polynesian cultures. According to the *Lonely Planet's Guide* website, "The Polynesian concept of family is a much broader one than in the west. Cousins, uncles, aunts are all part of the scene. . . . The family might also have adopted children . . . and children are commonly entrusted to relatives or childless women."[28]

In many of these societies there was no real sense of a child belonging to a set of parents. Rather, the children were frequently shared by many households so that an individual child might call many places home and many people parents. In Tahitian society, for example, the word for mother was also the same word for aunt or grandmother. In many early societies every member of a tribe was in some way related to one another.

Writer and world traveler Paul Theroux, on his journey through the Pacific Islands during the early 1990s, asked a Polynesian man why family was so important. The unnamed man's reply: "Because it helps you—it looks after you. It is your life."[29]

There were strict relationship rules within most families that guided behavior. These rules were particularly stringent between brothers and sisters. Anthropologist and writer Margaret Mead, the first twentieth century Westerner to report in detail on Polynesian societies, gave this description of the rules Samoan society imposed on brothers and sisters:

After they have reached . . . nine or ten years old . . . [they] may not touch each other, sit close together, address each other familiarly. They may not remain in any house except their own together unless half the village is gathered there. They may not walk together, use each other's possessions, dance on the same floor or take part in any of the same small group activities.[30]

Marriage

Throughout Pacific Island societies young people were expected to marry at an early age. Relatives usually arranged these marriages when the children were young. Elaborate wedding ceremonies were often held and, in nearly every society, there was some kind of "bride-price" involved.

In many highland villages of Papua New Guinea, for instance, it was and still is expected that a young man "buys" the girl he wants through the arrangement of a bride-price. In the 1980s famed oceanographic and underwater explorer Jacques-Yves Cousteau and his son, Jean-Michel, and a large crew of scientists and photographers, spent time in New Guinea studying the natives who lived there. According to Jean-Michel, "For the groom's family, the bride-price is an opportunity to demonstrate wealth and prestige. To establish good will between the two families, the groom's people offer somewhat more than they can afford, and the bride's people return half of what they receive."[31]

This bride-price usually included the exchange of pigs, the most prized possession among many of the people of Papua

A traditional ceremonial wedding dance is performed on the island of Moorea.

New Guinea and other islands of Melanesia. If the price was not high enough, the bride's family could call off the upcoming wedding. If the price was acceptable, a marriage ceremony was held.

Following a period of singing and dancing, the two families gathered and listened to speeches given by elder members of both families. The marriage ceremony was completed with a symbolic handing over of the bride. Two members of her family carried the bride around on their shoulders and then placed her on the shoulders of the groom's family. This ritual officially welcomed the bride into her new family.

In some areas of the Solomons the person or group giving the largest contribution to the bride-price was often given the op-tion to name or even adopt the first child. And in Samoa special carpenters often built the new couple a home. A sacred oven full of food was prepared and served to the marriage couple. In many societies the new bride would spend several weeks living with her mother-in-law so that the older woman could pass along that family's history along with special skills and wisdom.

Giving Birth

Mead reports in her first book that

Birthdays are of little account. . . . But for the birth itself of the baby of high rank, a great feast will be held. The first baby must always be born in the mother's village. For several months before the birth of the child, the father's relatives have brought gifts of food to the prospective mother, while the mother's female relatives have been busy making pure white bark cloth for baby clothes.[32]

During the actual birth the woman was usually attended by her relatives, while immediately afterward the newborn was handed over to a female relative of the father. A midwife was also present and was responsible for cutting the umbilical cord. Mead reports: "If the baby is a girl, the cord is buried under a paper mulberry tree to ensure her growing up to be industrious at household tasks; for a boy it is thrown into the sea that he may be a skilled fisherman or planted under a taro tree to give him industry in farming."[33]

In most areas of the Pacific, regardless of culture, babies were breast-fed for at least two or three years. If a woman became pregnant during that time, a wet nurse or another nursing mother would be utilized.

Children

The first-born child, regardless of sex, usually had the highest rank and greatest importance within a family. Children were seldom punished. Most parents believed that independent children would make better warriors and adult family members. Children acquired virtually all of their learning through play.

Boys often had less responsibility than girls because of the predominately male-oriented societies. Boys did few household chores; their primary tasks usually cen-

tered around learning the skills they would need as warriors and hunters. Thus, they spent most of their days hunting birds and other small animals, throwing spears, and wrestling with one another.

Girls had a much heavier household responsibility in order to prepare them for their roles as adult women. They usually helped their mothers prepare food, weed the garden, and gather paper mulberry bark to make into clothing. In addition, young girls six or seven years old were also used as babysitters for their younger siblings.

Young girls frequently began dancing lessons early in life. In New Zealand, for instance, Maori girls began their study of native dancing by twirling and spinning *poi* balls—tightly bound balls made of native plants that were attached to long cords. It was believed that these exercises would teach the girls a sense of rhythm and quickness that would be essential for them later in life.

Circumcision played an important part in a young boy's life on various islands in the Pacific. On the Melanesian island of Vanuatu, for instance, circumcision took place when a boy was five years old. Following the procedure the boy was sent into the wilderness for a period of two months, during which he was kept away from the tribe's women and cared for by male family members.

Initiation Rites: Polynesian Tattooing

While a young girl officially became a woman upon the completion of her first menstrual cycle, young boys throughout the Pacific were often required to undergo specific and often painful initiation rites prior to entering manhood.

In Polynesia, tattooing played the central role in the initiation of young boys. In New Zealand, for instance, Maori priests served not only as religious leaders but also were responsible for doing the sacred tattooing. Maori males had their entire faces tattooed, a process called *moko* that could take many weeks or even years to complete. Each facial design was unique and depicted details of a person's skills, achievements, or family history.

The *Lonely Planet's Guide* states that on Samoa,

> When a boy is born his grandmother will begin collecting dye for his tattoo and when a male is fully grown (twelve to fourteen years of age) he's taken to a *tufuga* [priest] who spends up to a month carving the youth in tattoos from waist to knee using shark's teeth. The process is incredibly painful and represents the strength of a man's heart and his spirituality.[34]

Initiation Rites: Melanesian Scarification

In Papua New Guinea, when a young man is ready to pass from childhood into manhood he undergoes a dramatic skin-cutting ceremony called scarification. According to the editors of National Geographic Books these complex rites "wash away the female impurities of childhood and

Sexuality

One of the things that attracted early European sailors and settlers to the Pacific Islands was the casual sexual practices they discovered there. Polynesian women, in particular, were very uninhibited and offered themselves freely to the white sailors.

Tahitian society was especially known for its sexual freedom. Teenagers, in fact, were not only allowed to have sex, but encouraged to do so. Children were taught about sexuality and sex at a very early age, and it was quite common throughout Tahiti for both girls and boys to mate promiscuously for many years before settling down to married life.

In many Polynesian cultures it was socially acceptable for married people to have sex with other partners. On most islands only two things were forbidden: incest, or having sex with family members, and having sex across class boundaries. If a commoner was found to be having sex with someone of a higher class, both individuals were usually put to death.

mark their introduction to manhood."[35] This skin-cutting ceremony is a very painful ritual that is still practiced today in parts of Papua New Guinea.

The night before a ceremony the initiates are given a traditional drink containing a mild narcotic that will help them endure

The Asaro Mudmen of Papua New Guinea

During a visit to Papua New Guinea by underwater explorers Jacques-Yves and Jean-Michel Cousteau, they and their crew had the opportunity to meet members of the Asaro tribe, a group who lived deep in the Papau New Guinea highlands.

According to Jean-Michel and Mose Richards in *Cousteau's Papua New Guinea Journey,* the Asaro mudmen were legendary warriors who, "wearing ghostly, pumpkin-sized clay masks, coated in pale mud, presented a horrific specter that had long intimidated other tribes."

The Asaro mudmen were infamous for the large numbers of rival tribesmen they had killed during their long his-

tory. Jean-Michel Cousteau spoke with an elder of the Asaro tribe, Atairu Kanisuo, who told him: "Before, when we had enemies at war with us, the people of this village would wear mud masks because it disguised them. We could attack a village and kill without being recognized. People thought we were ghosts and they would flee us. Our men chased the enemies, cutting off heads, burning down houses, and slaughtering pigs. When the missionaries came, we gave up a lot of traditions, but we held on to the tradition of the mud masks. We don't use them for killing, just for dancing."

A mudman of the Asaro tribe in Papua New Guinea wears an unsightly mask used to intimidate rival tribesmen.

the pain of the scarification rite. After ceremonial dancing the young men are brought into the community house to have their heads shaved. They must then leap over a fire and run through a gauntlet of men armed with sticks. While the initiates rush through, they are shielded from many of the blows by a family "protector" who has been chosen to accompany the young man on his path to manhood. According to an unnamed New Guinea tribesman, "We must hit the boys very hard so they really get stung. If we didn't do this, they wouldn't develop the bodies of men; they wouldn't grow tough and strong."[36]

The actual scarification ceremony begins with the naked initiate sitting atop an upside-down canoe while his protector holds his head and shoulders. One or two elders of the tribe will do the actual cutting. A razor blade is used in modern tribal society, while a sharpened bamboo stick was used in the past. A pattern is cut in the boy's skin until the entire chest, arms, back, and thighs have been scarified. Each village has its own distinctive pattern, all of which resemble the scales of a crocodile, an animal sacred to the Papuans.

After the scarification has been completed, the young men are helped to their feet and then carried outside on their protectors' shoulders and presented to the entire village. Following a period of dancing the young men return to the community house where they will stay for several weeks while their scars heal. During these weeks they will also be taught the traditions, stories, and secrets of their tribes.

Living in extended family communities, the indigenous people of the Pacific led very productive lives. With the relatively strict rules and taboos that guided them, each individual knew his or her role in society. These carefully defined ways of life would flourish for hundreds of years.

Chapter 4

Religion and Magic

Religion and spirituality were an important part of everyday life in the Pacific. The belief that people, animals, and even objects possessed a life force or spirit was universal among the islanders, who attributed miraculous and magical powers to inanimate objects such as plants, animals, trees, rivers, mountains, and sculpted objects.

A few indigenous beliefs were similar to those of the Judaeo-Christian tradition. For example, the *Lonely Planet's Guide* reports that "Many islanders [on Vanuatu] believed in a Creator Tahara who didn't sound too different from Jehovah; a Garden of Eden where the original man and woman ate fruit from the forbidden rose apple tree and fell from grace; and the demon Saratau, who neatly paralleled Satan."[37]

This similarity is not as apparent in other areas of the Pacific. On the Solomon Islands, for instance, writer Paul Theroux asked a Savo native where his people originated. The man answered: "We came from a bird. . . . The bird . . . laid an egg and woman came out."[38]

Indigenous Beliefs

The worship of ancestor spirits and supernatural beings was widespread among the people of the Pacific. Everyday life revolved around keeping the gods and spirits satisfied and happy. Historian David Howarth puts it this way: "People called on them for help or protection much as some Christians pray to saints."[39]

If the spirits were pleased with a person or a tribe, those individuals were believed to be in line for rewards of good luck and spiritual power. Unfortunately, the ancestor spirits and gods also were easy to anger, especially if a taboo or spiritual rule was broken. Often death, natural disaster, disease, or crop failure was interpreted as the result of angering the spirits.

Many Polynesian societies prayed to wise guardian spirits, called *amakua* in Hawaii, for strength and guidance. The tribes attempted to appease the gods by staging lavish festivals and rituals during which animals and humans were sacrificed. All such ceremonies, says historian

Goran Burenhult, "had one main object: to secure the support of the supernatural powers for the human society."[40]

Seasonal cycles also played a significant role in religious ceremonies and rituals. By performing the appropriate rituals and making the necessary offerings to the appropriate spirits, the indigenous people believed they could assure favorable hunting, fishing, and crop production.

Gods and Goddesses

Throughout the Pacific, writes Tony Wheeler, "There is a rich mythology, easily as complex as anything the ancient Greeks and Romans ever came up with, which includes a panoply of gods and explanations for all kinds of natural phenomena, including the creation of the earth and sky."[41]

For example, the editors of National Geographic Books report that the Tifalmin tribe of Papua New Guinea believed that, "In the beginning Afekan, the Heroine, the Creatress, lived that she might teach men how to live in strength and dignity. Through her wondrous powers she created the first taro and pigs and many items of culture."[42]

Tahitians called their supreme god *Te Atua* which simply means the "godhead" or "the concept of god." Research by the editors of Reader's Digest Books indicates that

A Hawaiian native makes an offering to appease the easily angered fire goddess, Pele.

Shark Worship and Calling

Many Pacific Island people worship the shark. On the island of Malaita in the Solomon Island chain, native Marcelline Saro told writer Paul Theroux of this reverence. The author recounts Saro's story in his book *The Happy Isles of Oceania.*

"My island is traditional [Melanesian] . . . we respect the shark, that is why we worship it. . . . And that is why we never eat the shark. We believe it will save us and protect us. . . . Every year we have the sacrifice ceremony of the roasted piglet. No woman may come near the altar ever. The shark caller summons the shark—he stands at the edge of the sea and calls the fish. When he sees it swimming towards him, he throws the piglet to it. And the shark eats it, and then protects us."

Other Pacific Island societies worshiped the shark during an annual religious ritual called "shark calling." On the island of Fiji a portion of a coral reef was marked off about a month before the actual shark calling to ensure that no one would fish or swim in that area. On the designated day the shark caller stood up to his neck in water and started chanting for the sharks to come. According to legend, when a school of sharks approached, the group was always led by one white shark. As the animals approached, the shark caller retreated to shore while the rest of the villagers speared the sharks as they came into the shallow water near the beach. This was a very dangerous activity but the people believed their ancestors would protect them from harm. In addition, by never killing the white shark, they believed they were assured of good hunting and safety.

A shark glides through the warm water that surrounds the Pacific Islands. Native Pacific Islanders believe these magnificent creatures protect them from harm.

"The chief deity of the peoples of western and central Polynesia was *Tangaroa,* god of navigators and the ocean. He was also believed to be the ancestor of the first people to arrive on [some of] the islands."[43]

In Hawaii, Pele, the goddess of volcanoes, was worshiped by the native Polynesians. Pele is usually portrayed as a tall and slender woman with long blond hair. She has always been characterized as a very jealous goddess. Traditional belief holds that frequent gifts are necessary to prevent her from becoming angry.

Magic and Sorcery

The belief in magic and the use of sorcery was common throughout the Pacific. It was in Melanesia, however, that these practices controlled nearly every aspect of daily life. According to Robert C. Kiste, such customs are still alive: "There are magical spells to ensure the growth of crops, bring success in fishing, guarantee victory in war and cure sickness."[44]

There was little distinction between magic and religion for the people of Melanesia. The islanders blamed virtually all bad luck and calamity on sorcery and the work of magic spirits. Some indigenous groups in Papua New Guinea, for example, believed that one supernatural power—Saia—was an evil force who caused accidents, sickness, and death. Saia could easily take possession of an item such as a boulder and cause it to fall and injure a climber.

Sorcerers were individuals who believed to have magical powers including the ability to cast evil spells on unsuspecting victims. There were many confirmed reports of people dying for no discernible reason other than fear stemming from the belief that sorcerers had the power over life and death. In many such cases the victim simply stopped eating and waited for death to come.

Many tribes in Papua New Guinea believed, according to journalist Tim Cahill, who spent time in that country visiting many different tribes, "during sleep . . . a man is most vulnerable to the evil influence of the spirit world. Therefore, it [was] wise to keep a skull nearby during sleep. Men formerly slept . . . using the powerful skulls of their ancestors, or their enemies, as pillows."[45]

Many indigenous people carried special objects such as rocks, teeth, and feathers to ward off evil spirits. In Fiji, for example, one of the most sacred traditions was the presentation of a carefully polished whale tooth, or *tabua,* to visiting dignitaries. Fijians believed that the *tabua* was the home of ancestor spirits. *Tabua* were often buried with a person to ensure that the individual had a safe passage to the afterworld.

Shamans and Priests

As was true of other indigenous cultures around the world, the people of the Pacific relied on shamans or medicine men for the proper performance of many religious and spiritual rituals. Shamans usually held a position of honor in native society and were said to possess incredible spiritual power.

There were two ways of becoming a shaman. One was to be selected by elder members of a tribe and then trained in the necessary spells, songs, prayers, and ceremonies. The other way was to have a vision or dream in which the spirits sent a personal message telling a young man that he was to become a shaman. Both of these events usually took place during childhood.

The role model for the Hawaiian shaman was the great culture hero and god, Maui. Shamanic expert Shirley Nicholson writes: "Among other things, Maui was known for such shamanistic practices as turning himself into various animals and birds, being helped by animals and birds, visiting the heavens to gain the secrets of fire and cultivation . . . and exploring the underworld."[46]

Shamans interacted with the spirits in very personal ways. Usually this involved going into a trance, during which the shaman was thought to travel to another realm where the answers to certain questions could be found. Many shamans also used the trance method to help treat patients believed to be suffering from spirit possession or sorcery.

In addition to summoning "magical" powers to heal the sick, shamans often prescribed herbs and other plant materials to alleviate symptoms. Taro was one of the most common plants used by shamans in the Pacific. A thickened concoction of taro was often used as a poultice on infected wounds, while the actual leaf stalk could be rubbed on insect bites

The Use of Myths

As is true of many indigenous people throughout the world, the Pacific Islanders used myths and legends to explain nearly every facet of their lives. Stories were used to explain the presence of the sun and moon, the existence of animals, and the origin of many natural elements. The Fijians passed down the following story about how the beautiful Tagimaucia flower got its red color.

"A woman and her young daughter lived high on a hill. One day the mother called the child over to help her with the chores, but the young girl kept on playing. Angry, the mother hit the little girl with a broom and told her to go away and never come back. The youngster was broken hearted and, with tears running down her cheeks, ran deep into the forest.

Unable to see where she was going because of her crying, she ran into a large climbing plant and quickly became tangled up in its thick vines. Unable to break free, the girl cried harder and harder until her tears turned to blood. Where the girl's tears touched the green vine, they were suddenly transformed into beautiful red flowers.

After a long struggle the girl was finally able to break free. She ran straight home, where she found her mother waiting with open arms. The two lived happily ever after—and from that time on, the lovely red flowers called Tagimaucia have bloomed on the vine."

to take away the sting and itch. In addition, taro juice, when blended with sugar or coconut milk, was useful in reducing fever. The root itself was given to stop bleeding. There are no statistics available to determine how effective these treatments really were, but scientists speculate that anti-inflammatory agents within the taro plant may have produced partial relief of symptoms.

Priests performed many of the same functions that shamans did but also served their tribes in other ways. In Hawaii, for instance, it was the priest or kahuna who established the religious laws and taboos. Priests were also responsible for finding and then blessing a place where a sacred temple or other religious structure was to be built. The priest was called in to determine if the land was appropriate for spiritual use. He accomplished this by reading certain signs in nature including the energy of a specific location. The priest also consulted various spirits and made readings of cloud formations and the stars.

In New Zealand the Maoris had a priestly class called the *tohungas* who, according to writer Tony Wheeler, "were charged with keeping the history, genealogy, stories, and spiritual matters of the tribe."[47]

A Papuan shaman stands beside sacred painted skulls displayed on an altar to ward off evil spirits.

Illness and Death

Many indigenous people believed in life after death. The Solomon Islanders, for instance, believed that a person's spirit lived on, for a time, in animals. It was a common belief that sharks and birds were actually the ghosts of dead people. For that reason the bereaved family would refrain from eating that particular animal for a period of time after the death of a loved one.

Other natives believed that the dead went to live with various gods. Several tribes in Papua New Guinea worshiped Nutu, the Master of All Things. In death,

Sacred Places

In addition to the temples and spirit houses found throughout the Pacific, there are many other places that are still sacred to the indigenous people. Perhaps the most famous of these is Nan Madol, one of the most remarkable religious centers built in the Pacific.

Homes for the nobility, tombs, and ceremonial buildings dominated Nan Madol, at one time a floating city on Pohnpei Island in Micronesia. Built somewhere between the tenth and thirteenth centuries, this religious center spanned nearly one hundred small islands and was connected by a network of manmade canals. The structure now lies hidden by dense jungle.

There are several sacred sites in Hawaii. Perhaps the best known is Haleakala Crater on the island of Maui. According to *National Geographic* writer Cynthia Russ Ramsay in her book *Hawaii's Hidden Treasures,* "the crater is dotted with prehistoric cairns [piles of rocks], platforms and rock shelters. . . . In the past, Hawaiians came to the crater to inter the bones of their dead . . . and perform ceremonies."

And in the Waipi'o Valley on the big island of Hawaii, on certain trails hikers are still cautioned not to go to sleep. It is believed that the ghosts of great warrior chieftains come back to earth at night and march along the paths. Some people even claim to have seen a torchlight procession of these night marchers.

they believed that their relatives' souls went to live with this god.

The indigenous people of the Pacific believed that magic and sorcery caused illness and death. In addition, the natives of Polynesia also looked at the attitudes of one's relatives as a possible factor during times of troubles. In her book about the people of Samoa, anthropologist Margaret Mead wrote:

If an individual falls ill, the explanation is sought first in the attitude of his relatives. Anger in the heart of a relative, especially in that of a sister,

is most potent in producing evil. . . . The whole household is convened . . . and each relative is solemnly enjoined to confess what anger there is in his heart against the sick person.[48]

It was believed, as well, that the breaking of taboos could bring on illness or catastrophe. On the islands of Hawaii, for instance, the catching and eating of certain fish was forbidden at certain times of the year. If an individual or a tribe broke this taboo and poor fishing or sickness followed, the pairing of events reinforced the Hawaiians' belief in the power of taboos. Offenders were generally punished and a period of stricter adherence to the rules ensued.

When death occurred after illness, many tribes in Papua New Guinea took revenge on a scapegoat. Tim Cahill explains by noting that, "a death is believed to be caused by witchcraft and a culprit (scapegoat) must be found, killed and eaten by the relatives in revenge."[49]

Honoring the Dead

Funeral rituals differed widely among the various indigenous people of the Pacific. Some tribes buried their dead, others cremated the bodies, and yet others performed elaborate funeral ceremonies. The Huli tribe of New Guinea, for example, honored their dead by painting their skulls and bones and placing them in a special family vault made of stone.

Edward Marriott reports that another tribe in Papua New Guinea, the Hagahai, "laid out their dead on scaffolds, storing the bones . . . in a cave or in a high tree; widows kept their husbands' jawbones as mementos."[50] In the Samoa Islands, on the other hand, dead ancestors were simply buried in the family garden.

During his travels journalist Tim Cahill visited the traditional village of Syuru in New Guinea and observed the funeral ceremony of an important villager. He writes, "The women had covered their bodies with ashes and soot. They would mourn . . . for several days. . . . Wailing and moaning would build to a crescendo."[51] The moaning and wailing constituted a sign of respect intended to make a favorable impression on the spirits and to prevent the dead person from returning as a ghost.

A Maori funeral is called a *tangihanga*. Even in twenty-first-century New Zealand, many age-old practices are still followed. Family and friends gather around an open and simple wooden coffin for several days prior to the burial. Many of the older family members give speeches commemorating the person's life. The elders also pay tribute and pray to many different ancestor spirits. After the relatives dig the grave,

Mourners honor a deceased family member at a Papuan funeral ritual.

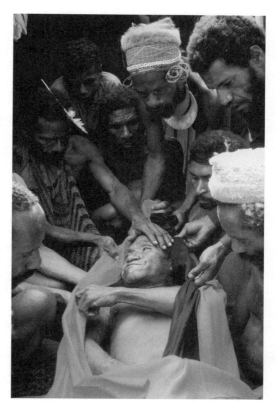

the person is laid to rest along with a large selection of personal belongings.

Temples and Spirit Houses

The indigenous people of the Pacific built many different kinds of temples, spirit houses, and other structures dedicated for religious purposes. A Polynesian temple was called a *marae,* and was usually characterized by a stone altar. Other stones or statues were located within the structure to represent different ancestors, deities, or important living individuals within the tribe.

Most Polynesian families had their own individual *marae* and used them for praying to the spirits of their deceased relatives. Pigs and other animals were often sacrificed to the spirits within these enclosures. Tribal chiefs built larger and more elaborate *marae* throughout Polynesia. Historian Goran Burenhult reports that according to native belief, "Human sacrifice was necessary during the construction of the royal *marae.* An individual chosen by the chief was attacked and clubbed to death, after which the remains were carried to the [spiritual] center in a basket."[52]

The spirit house in Papua New Guinea is called a *haus tambaran* and is an exclusively male sanctuary. A *haus* is an impressive structure that often juts high into the sky. The village's sacred and magical objects have for centuries been kept within these sacred buildings.

During his stay in Papua New Guinea, *National Geographic* writer Francois Ley-det was invited into a *haus tambaran* belonging to the Palimbei natives. Leydet describes it as

> a long two-storied building faced with intricately woven matting, the roof thatched, and soaring to a peak at either end. On the ground floor, men sat on platforms smoking twist tobacco or chewing betel nut. . . . Grotesquely beautiful, eerily powerful carved masks and figures stared at me from the ceiling beams and columns. On the second floor, initiation ceremonies are held.[53]

In Fiji huge temples called *naga* were built in the form of stone enclosures, while the Hawaiians built ritual centers called *heiau.* Both of these structures were used for ceremonial and religious purposes.

The Statues of Easter Island

When a Dutch ship landed on a previously "undiscovered" island on Easter Sunday in 1722, the sailors were astonished to see the shore lined with giant stone statues. Some fifty years later legendary British explorer Captain James Cook, upon landing on Easter Island, would write: "We could hardly conceive how these islanders, totally unacquainted with any mechanical power, could raise such stupendous figures."[54]

The generally accepted theory is that these majestic stone statues were erected to honor various Polynesian gods and ancestor spirits. The human-shaped statues, called *moai,* have been found nowhere else in the entire Pacific region. The *moai* are gigantic,

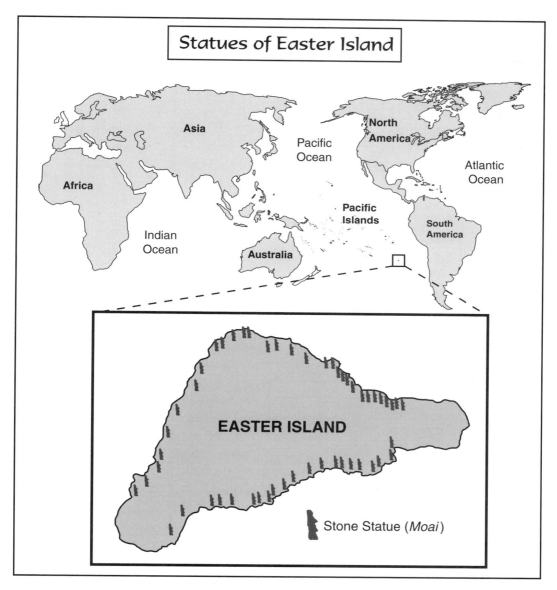

Statues of Easter Island

EASTER ISLAND

█ Stone Statue (*Moai*)

most ranging in height from twelve to twenty feet and weighing an average of eighteen tons or more. No two *moai* are exactly alike, but all have common features. They have elongated fingers, large noses and ears, narrow lips, and deep eye sockets.

Each of the great statues sits on a stone platform called an *ahu*. Some of the *ahu* appear to be large altars, while others were used as burial chambers. The nearly one thousand statues found on Easter Island were built at the height of the native

Mysteriously erected by natives in honor of Polynesian gods and spirits, the moai *(stone statues) line the coast of Easter Island.*

created a work of art that continues to astound and amaze visitors today.

According to those who have seen them, the statues, which all face inland, seem to be guarding the land. Many of the *moai* wear special "hats" called *pukao* made of cylindrical blocks of red stone. Hats, for the Rapa Nui, were signs of prestige and grandeur and were worn or given only to high-ranking nobles or chiefs. It is thought that the hats were added to provide extra protection for the family or clan that erected the statue.

Unfortunately, no written account exists that fully describes the statues in all their grandeur. By the time the Europeans arrived, the statues lay in ruins, destroyed by the islanders during tribal warfare or, according to one intriguing theory, because the gods the *moai* represented were believed to have failed. In the twenty-first century, however, many of the statues have been restored and together they are called *aringa ora* or "living faces."

For hundreds of years the indigenous people of the Pacific followed their various spiritual practices in relative peace and isolation. Beginning in the sixteenth century their ways of life and their belief systems would begin to crumble as they came in contact with unwelcome outsiders.

Rapa Nui culture, sometime between A.D. 400 and 1600. The statues were carved from volcanic rock and somehow—archaeologists still do not know exactly how—transported to the cliffs near the coast. Using only stone chisels, the carvers

Chapter 5

The Rediscovery of the Pacific Islands

The exploration of the Pacific by Europeans officially began with the discovery of the Pacific Ocean in 1513 by Spanish explorer Vasco Nuñez de Balboa. Seven years later another Spaniard, Ferdinand Magellan, would be the first European to sail across that vast body of water. Not until the late sixteenth and early seventeenth centuries, however, would Europeans begin their historic voyages of discovery.

It was the Dutch who then took the lead in exploring the Pacific. "Abel Tasman," according to historian Robert C. Kiste, "contributed more knowledge about the Pacific than any other European up to his time."[55] Tasman is credited with the discovery of New Zealand, Tonga, and parts of Fiji. Another Dutchman, Jacob Roggeveen, would land on Easter Island in 1722.

The primary French explorer was Louis Antoine de Bougainville, the first Westerner to visit Tahiti, Samoa, New Guinea, and the Solomon Islands. Despite the success of the Dutch and French, however, it was the British who dominated the era of

major European exploration. During the latter part of the eighteenth century, the English were led by Captain James Cook, cited by historians as the greatest of all European explorers to visit the Pacific. Cook is credited with the discovery of the Cook Islands and Hawaii. The great era of discovery, despite a few explorations in the early nineteenth century, would end with Cook's murder in Hawaii in 1779.

Reaction to the Europeans

Because there were no written languages among the many peoples of the Pacific, historians rely on information from Europeans and also native legends to describe the early reactions to the strange-looking newcomers. A Hawaiian scholar, Samuel Kamakua, tells the following story about the first European landing in Hawaii:

> The first to see Cook's two ships were two Kauai fishermen out in the night in their canoes. Startled to see [the ships] loom up out of the darkness, they made the immediate

surmise that these were the two floating islands on which the god Lono had promised that he would one day reappear. . . . Awed and terrified, the fishermen fled home . . . to tell what they had seen.[56]

By morning the shores were lined with hundreds of natives. As the ships approached, shouts of excitement echoed throughout the land. A priest and a chief went out in a canoe to greet the arriving "god." Cook would later record in his diary that "all fell flat on their faces and remained in that humble posture till . . . I made the signs for them to rise."[57]

The belief that the newcomers were returning gods was a common theme throughout the Pacific Islands. Even as late as the 1930s this belief held true in Papua New Guinea. Jean-Michael Cousteau and Mose Richards report evidence of the legend's persistence:

On the morning of May 27, 1930 . . . two gold prospectors from Australia . . . walked into a highland valley of . . . Papua New Guinea and discovered . . . a previously unknown civilization of nearly one million people who had never before had contact with the outside world. . . . [The natives] assumed

An artist's illustration of a Hawaiian battle scene depicting the death of European explorer Captain James Cook (pointing in foreground), famous for his eighteenth-century discovery of the Cook Islands and Hawaii.

that the two pale figures in khaki shorts . . . were ancestral spirits returned from the dead.[58]

Two Devastating Forces

By bringing guns and disease to the South Pacific, whalers and early explorers unleashed devastating forces on the defenseless islanders. The introduction of guns to native cultures led to increasing violence and lethal intertribal warfare. Those chiefs who possessed these weapons were able to inflict heavy casualties on their enemies. As a result, indigenous populations began to decline in numbers.

Far more devastating than guns, however, was disease. Living isolated on the remote islands for centuries, the indigenous people of the Pacific had no immunity against the diseases they were exposed to by the Europeans. Smallpox, measles, influenza, tuberculosis, and venereal disease spread like wildfire through the various islands and decimated entire populations. A nineteenth-century measles outbreak killed over half the population of Fiji.

Sexual encounters between island women and European sailors left thousands of women pregnant. These encounters also introduced various forms of sexually transmitted diseases such as syphilis and gonorrhea into the native population. Unable to treat these maladies, many indigenous people died.

Influenza was another particularly devastating disease that affected the Pacific Island natives. In the early twentieth century a massive flu epidemic swept the world, resulting in the deaths of millions. The people of Samoa acquired the disease in a particularly tragic manner. On November 7, 1918, a ship arrived in Samoa from New Zealand. Government officials knew that many members of the crew were infected with the influenza virus. No quarantine of the ship, however, was ordered, despite common knowledge that the disease was highly contagious. Tens of thousands of Samoans became sick and over one-fifth of the population died, leaving a legacy of mistrust and hard feelings toward New Zealand that endures to this day.

The Growth of Trade

Europeans found rich and bountiful lands when they landed on the various islands in the Pacific. Within a few short years traders and merchants were exploiting the islands' riches. Traders were looking for such goods as coconut oil, sandalwood, and pearl shells. Trading communities and port cities quickly developed on many of the larger islands. Because the Hawaiian Islands were perfectly positioned for all kinds of shipping, every powerful European country and the United States had a presence there. By the early nineteenth century Honolulu had become a major port for international whalers and traders.

Sandalwood was a particularly lucrative item found on many of the islands. A rich and fragrant wood, sandalwood had long been a valued product in China where it was used in incense. While the sandalwood trade did not last long, it nonetheless had dire

Leprosy

A particularly devastating illness was carried to Hawaii from Asia in the 1860s. Called *mai pake*, the "Chinese malady," this very contagious disease affects the skin and nerves, leading frequently to a horrible death. Now called leprosy or Hansen's disease, the illness swept through the Hawaiian Islands, killing thousands of Polynesians.

The Hawaiian government, with the help of American advisers, chose to remove all infected natives to an isolated compound on the island of Molokai. In the years that followed, Father Joseph Damien de Veuster, a Belgian priest, moved to the island to care for the lepers. Much beloved by the natives, Father Damien would

eventually die of the same disease.

With the advent of modern drugs and medicine, leprosy is not the problem it once was, although there is still a small leper colony on Molokai today.

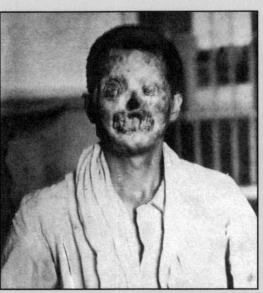

A leper in China. Leprosy is highly contagious, leaves its victims grossly disfigured, and without treatment leads to an agonizing death.

consequences. In Hawaii, King Kamehameha I forced his subjects to cut down most of the islands' sandalwood. There and in other places, heavy overcutting of trees quickly depleted the supply of this resource. In addition, because most of the islanders were busy cutting timber, native crops were neglected and often entirely abandoned, contributing to the breakdown of ancient ways of life.

Europeans were also extremely interested in copra or coconut oil. By the mid–nineteenth century there was a growing demand in Europe for tropical vegetable oils. This often led to the building of huge plantations which altered the landscape on many islands, disrupting the ecological balance as well.

The Missionaries

Close on the heels of the explorers and traders, hundreds of Christian missionaries sailed for the Pacific. There was much that shocked mid-nineteenth-century Westerners—practices long banished from Europe and North America: paganism, nudity, and illiteracy.

The London Missionary Society was among the first to send missionaries to the Pacific. "In 1797," according to the editors of Reader's Digest Books, "shocked by tales of cannibalism, promiscuity, human sacrifice . . . the London Missionary Society . . . landed missionaries in Tahiti, the Marquesas and Tonga."[59] By the 1850s and 1860s missionaries were hard at work on nearly every island in the Pacific.

Thus fortified with the belief that they were bringing not only religious salvation but also humanitarian practices and Western habits of dressing to the local populations, Roman Catholic and Protestant missionaries flocked to the area. Writes Robert C. Kiste: "Missions provided education and, in some cases, modest medical care."[60] Intertribal warfare and cannibalism were stamped out on many islands. Thousands of islanders turned to Christianity while managing to retain many of their traditional practices.

In contrast to the benefits—and, in the opinion of some, outweighing them—were the terrible effects of the missionaries' narrow-mindedness and cultural insensitivity. The various cultures, writes Tony Wheeler, found "themselves spiritually assaulted and much of their tradition and culture irrevocably altered."[61] Children who attended missionary schools were forbidden to speak their native tongues and punished for violating the rule. As a result, many societies disintegrated, a great deal of traditional heritage was lost, and innumerable changes occurred in the lives of the people. Missionaries in New Guinea also destroyed vast treasuries of native art. This was especially true along the Sepik River, a region that has been recognized by museums and art collectors as one of the richest sources of primitive art in the world.

How the Missionaries Changed Island Society

British journalist Edward Marriott, who lived among a tribe in the highlands of Papua New Guinea, reports that missionary techniques were similar throughout the Pacific: "Rule by fear, reading matter restricted to the Bible, baptism alone averting damnation."[62] Marriott continues in this critical vein by writing, "Rare were missionaries who respected indigenous beliefs."[63]

Missionaries quickly realized that the key to converting large numbers of people was first to persuade the various tribal chiefs to adopt Christianity. Once the chiefs had publicly acknowledged their new belief, the rest of the village soon followed. In order to persuade the chiefs to convert, the missionaries were willing to use almost any enticement. If gifts of food and clothing failed to obtain results, the missionaries, often working hand in hand with colonial governments, offered bribes of guns and machinery. These items were much coveted by the chiefs, who could use them to enhance their own positions of power.

The missionaries, however, retained considerable power of their own, setting up stringent rules and regulations and enforcing them with punishment and occasionally imprisonment. On many islands police forces were established. Known as *rikos* on the Cook Islands, the police were charged with reporting any cultural "offenses" among the island population. Such acts ranged from the performance of traditional dances to the failure to show proper respect for Westerners.

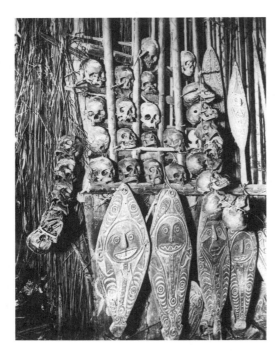

Stacks of skulls line the wall in a headhunter's tomb. These trophies, accompanied by the shields of the deceased, were used to flaunt the number of victims killed by the headhunter.

The missionaries were openly scornful of native religions, believing that by eliminating rites and ceremonies that had bound the people together for centuries, they were doing the islanders a favor. In many places missionaries leveled temples, banned certain initiation rites, destroyed sacred carvings, and forbade dancing.

In Hawaii, missionaries banned the hula. Rachel Naki of Hawaii remembers the days of the missionaries very well. Born during the early years of the twentieth century, Naki told *National Geographic* journalist Cynthia Russ Ramsay, "Those days very strict. You cannot dance the hula. If you sing hula song you gonna get a hundred sticks on your backside."[64]

By the latter part of the nineteenth century Christianity prevailed throughout most of the Pacific. In many respects the new religion fitted in well with the islanders' taste for ceremony and ritual. Often, however, the people fought against attempts to impose another set of beliefs and devotional practices. Many missionaries lost their lives at the hands of the indigenous people of the Pacific. Perhaps the most famous case is that of the Reverend Thomas Baker, who so offended and angered the Fijians that they killed and ate him in 1867. The only part of him that remained was one shoe, which is now exhibited in the Fiji Museum.

Why Did the Europeans Settle the Pacific?

The early European explorers, traders, and missionaries not only had a tremendous impact on the various indigenous peoples

Kamehameha

Kamehameha (1758–1819) was one of the greatest and best known of all Polynesian rulers. In his youth the young warrior had been the first and only chief ever to lift Hilo's famous Naha Stone, a huge boulder that today is located in front of the Hilo Public Library on the big island of Hawaii. According to ancient legends, any individual who could lift this immense stone would one day rule and unite all the islands of Hawaii. It took Kamehameha just nine years to fulfill the legend's prophecy. With the help of white adventurers and their modern guns, Kamehameha, from 1782 to 1791, gradually conquered the islands one by one.

He was a much beloved ruler, but perhaps his greatest achievement was his welcoming of trade with the Europeans while at the same time retaining firm control of his country. Proclaiming himself king, Kamehameha created laws against murder and other crimes, and encouraged his people to increase food production.

Early on the morning of May 8, 1819, the king drew his last breath. A pig was offered to the gods to ensure Kamehameha's entrance into the realm of gods, from whom the people believed he was descended. The memory and exploits of King Kamehameha are still celebrated in modern Hawaii. Statues of the great king can be found throughout the islands, while every June a lavish state holiday is held, complete with festivals and parades. Noted for his leadership and great physical strength, King Kamehameha still holds a special place in the hearts of native Hawaiians.

A statue of King Kamehameha is decorated with leis on Kamehameha Day, April 12, in Honolulu, Hawaii.

of the Pacific, but their written and verbal accounts of their life in the islands also captured the imagination of Westerners. According to Robert C. Kiste, "The reports of such early explorers as James Cook . . . inflamed the imagination of Europeans and Americans. The kingdoms of Polynesian chiefs and the trappings of their courts were colorful and impressive. The relative ease of life, the seemingly endless bounty of tropical islands, and the accounts of casual sexuality had tremendous impact."[65]

Living conditions in the early part of the nineteenth century were extremely poor in Europe. Many thousands of people labored in sweatshops for little money. As word of the islands reached the newly industrialized nations of the world, hundreds and then thousands of individuals began to look toward the Pacific as a place to make a new start. Land was plentiful there and the atmosphere much more pleasant than the smoke-filled cities and factories of Europe.

Colonists initially avoided the islands of Melanesia and New Guinea. Rain forests, thick jungles, mountains, and hordes of mosquitoes were among the factors that delayed settlement on these islands. The Europeans were also discouraged because of the hostile reputations of the indigenous people who were found to be ferocious headhunters and cannibals. As a result, it would be late into the nineteenth century before any serious attempts were made to set up trading posts in Melanesia and New Guinea. The islands of Micronesia were also avoided. Useful only as a stopover for whaling and trading vessels, these islands lacked Western settlements until the mid–nineteenth century.

The Seizure of Native Lands

To accommodate the tens of thousands of Europeans who began to sail toward the Pacific, massive amounts of land were needed. Throughout the islands colonial governments began to seize land from the people who lived there. Land, formerly used for individual or community gardens, was taken and turned into large plantations, while timber, which was in short supply in Europe, was cut without thought of replacement. Large areas of virgin forest simply disappeared from the landscape forever.

The indigenous people of the Pacific had no real concept of land ownership. Unable to read or write, the islanders could not grasp the idea that marks on a piece of paper could be used to deprive them of their land. The Europeans unscrupulously took advantage of the natives' unfamiliarity with business practices that had been standard elsewhere in the world for centuries. When the islanders offered resistance, the Westerners turned to violence to obtain the land they desired.

Throughout the Pacific, Europeans found ways to seize large amounts of land from the unsuspecting natives. In the Solomon Islands, for instance, British commissioner Charles Morris Woodford was charged with protecting the small contingent of Europeans who lived there. He also took it upon himself to increase his own profit by selling land.

To avoid any charges of wrongdoing, Woodford sailed around the islands labeling apparently unowned or unused land as "wasteland." However, much of this land was communally owned by the islanders and it was being "rested" in adherence to the traditional practice of shifting planting areas every few years. Woodford seized this unoccupied land, which in fact was understood by local residents to be community property, and sold it to new settlers, making huge profits. His actions led to troubling land rights issues that persist in the Solomons today.

The methods employed by Woodford were not unique to the Solomon Islands.

Unscrupulous Western governments and colonists throughout the nineteenth century simply took what land they wanted, leaving the people without the benefit of their land and disrupting their way of life. The island populations had little choice

Captain James Cook

James Cook (1728–1779) was one of the most famous explorers in history. While he made voyages to the North Atlantic and Pacific Northwest, he is best known for his three great voyages of discovery to the Pacific Ocean.

Cook was born in Great Britain, where he eventually enlisted in the Royal Navy and spent his early career years exploring the North Atlantic waters off Canada and the United States. In 1768 Cook commanded the ship *Endeavour* and made his first voyage to the South Pacific. On this journey he and his men landed on the eastern coast of Australia and also took possession of the island of New Zealand on behalf of Great Britain.

In 1773 on yet another voyage, he discovered the Cook Islands, which were later named in his honor. He also charted New Hebrides, the Marquesas, Easter Island, and New Caledonia. In July 1776 he set forth on his final voyage. He and his crew discovered the Hawaiian Islands. Cook named these new lands the Sandwich Islands after one of his sponsors, the earl of Sandwich. During a second stopover in

Hawaii in 1779 he was honored by the natives and taken to a high temple where a great feast had been planned for him.

This visit, however, ended tragically. Cook was infuriated when one of his rowboats was stolen by the Polynesians and in retaliation, tried to capture the local chief to hold as hostage until the boat was returned. A fight erupted during which Cook and several of his sailors were killed. The date was February 14, 1779.

Captain James Cook is best known for his three historic voyages of discovery to the Pacific.

A pineapple crop on the island of Hawaii. It was common for European settlers to hire Pacific Islanders to work on their plantations.

but to submit to the overwhelming power arrayed against them.

The Growth of the Plantation System in the Pacific

Many Westerners began almost immediately to turn this newly acquired land into large plantations that grew everything from sugarcane to coconuts to pineapples. Needing large amounts of labor to work these huge tracts of land, Europeans turned to the local people.

Unscrupulous tactics were often used to recruit plantation workers and many were forced to leave their home islands for work elsewhere in the Pacific. Many died during their years overseas; others chose to stay on the new islands; some opted to return home. For thousands of islanders, their years of working on the plantations became an accepted passage and initiation into adulthood.

Adjustment to plantation life was difficult for the Pacific Islanders. There was no common language, and this led to frequent misunderstandings between the islanders and their white overseers. In addition, former intertribal enemies were often required to work side by side, creating constant tension and violence. A fundamental problem arose because of the vast differences between indigenous and European customs. Islanders who had been members of the traditional nobility found themselves being treated as slaves and often whipped and humiliated by their new masters.

In Papua New Guinea, for instance, the Papuans were required to call all white people by the pidgin names of either "masta" or "misis." They were also expected to stand up when spoken to and were instructed to step aside when meeting Europeans on the streets. While some owners treated the natives with a degree of kindness and respect, most islanders were forced to work long hours and were frequently mistreated.

Plantation owners, for the most part, found Polynesians and Micronesians to be inefficient workers, as thousands found ways to avoid the long and monotonous routines of daily plantation life. Many simply left the plantations and returned to their villages, while others faked illness and injury or simply slowed down their level of work. For these reasons and because warfare and disease had diminished indigenous populations, European owners often imported their laborers from far away. In Hawaii, Japanese, Chinese, and Filipino laborers were recruited; and in Fiji, East Indians were brought in to work on the sugar plantations. The conflict between Fijians and Indians continues to this day.

By the mid–nineteenth century, the exploration of the Pacific had ceased. Traders, whalers, missionaries, merchants, and plantation owners all had made their impacts on indigenous society. Island life was changing dramatically. The undercurrents were in place for a radical new development that would dominate island life for the next one hundred years. The era of colonialism was about to begin.

Chapter 6

From Colonialism to Independence

Prior to 1840 only Spain, which claimed the Marianas and Guam, and the Dutch, who held part of New Guinea, had firm control of any Pacific Islands. Great Britain acquired New Zealand in 1840, setting off a race by the Western powers to acquire colonies in the Pacific.

By the beginning of the twentieth century the islands and the best land holdings were in the hands of white colonists and governments. Native chiefs lost their prestige, clans were separated from their traditional homelands, and many native cultures had nearly disintegrated.

There was little thought given to allowing the indigenous people of the Pacific to control their own destinies. According to historian Ruth M. Tabrah, "[The late nineteenth] century was an era in which independence and self-government for such peoples as the Hawaiians [and others] was not an alternative considered . . . by colonial empires."[66]

Trouble in Paradise

On islands all across the Pacific indigenous people resisted the takeover of their islands by European settlers and their governments. Conflict and violence were common with large-scale wars breaking out in several places. The biggest uprising took place on the island of New Zealand.

With increased hostility developing between British settlers and the native Maori, Great Britain in 1840 negotiated the Treaty of Waitangi. This document guaranteed the Maori that the English would not touch the lands owned by the natives. In return the Maori agreed to grant sovereignty to Queen Victoria. Before the ink on the treaty was dry, however, the British were violating the agreement by seizing large amounts of land.

Disturbed by this obvious violation of the treaty, the Maoris put aside their tribal differences and united to fight against the British. The Maori Wars of the 1850s and 1860s resulted in a tremendous loss of native life—and land. Writes Tony Wheeler,

"Although the Maori were brilliant warriors, eventually they were worn down by sheer weight of numbers and equipment."[67] The end of this war saw the end of widespread resistance against the forces of British colonialism.

Violence also occurred on many other Pacific Islands as numerous indigenous groups rebelled against the European powers that wanted to gain control of their homelands. A revolt occurred on the island of New Caledonia in the late 1870s. "To prevent another insurrection," writes historian Donald Seekins, "French authorities instituted the *indigenat,* an administrative system that deprived the Melanesians of the protection of the law and put them under the control of officials who had great latitude in imposing fines and punishment."[68]

Colonial governments and their soldiers dealt harshly with any evidence of rebellion. For example, on April 8, 1841, eighty officers and enlisted men from the American vessel USS *Peacock* descended on a village in Kiribati, leaving massive destruction in their wake. The *Lonely Planet's*

The Treaty of Waitangi

On many islands of the Pacific, Europeans simply bought or took native land without firing a shot or presenting a treaty. The situation was a bit different on the island of New Zealand, but the result was essentially the same.

The Treaty of Waitangi was put into effect on February 6, 1840. Among other things, this treaty asked that the Maori recognize the British Parliament and Queen Victoria as their rulers. In exchange, the Maori would be granted the same rights and privileges of citizenship as the people of England. The treaty also guaranteed to the Maori full possession of their land for as long as they wanted.

The Maoris were at a serious disadvantage because important sections of the treaty were not clearly explained. They did not, for instance, understand that the British retained the right to sell Maori land to future settlers. By the end of the nineteenth century most of the natives' land had been taken from them.

In the latter part of the twentieth century various Maori leaders in New Zealand began pressing for justice for these land seizures. The Waitangi Tribunal was formed in 1975 to investigate what had happened. Since that time a number of financial reparations have been made to several different Maori tribes whose land had been unjustly confiscated. The Tainui tribe, for instance, in 1975 received $175 million for land taken from their ancestors. The government of New Zealand hopes to settle all claims by the year 2010.

The Americans forced Hawaiian king Ka'lakaua to agree to a new constitution giving up most of the king's power.

Guide provides details: "They believed the locals had killed one of their number . . . and . . . they burned three hundred houses and left the community meeting house . . . entirely in ashes as their punishment."[69]

Overthrow of the Hawaiian Monarchy

From the beginning of U.S. involvement in Hawaii in the early 1800s, the various kings and nobles had dealt fairly and generously with the Americans. As increasing amounts of Hawaiian land fell under the control of rich American plantation owners, various wealthy businessmen began to advise Hawaiian monarchs and play a more active role in native government. The *haoles,* a Hawaiian word for foreigners, had become so powerful, in fact, that in 1887 they forced King Ka'lakaua to accept a new constitution that greatly decreased his power as king.

When the king died in 1891 he was succeeded by his sister Princess Lydia Lili'uokalani. The new queen came to power during an economic and political crisis in Hawaii. Her first goal was to restore the old constitution and return power to the throne. This proposed resumption of the monarchy posed a grave economic and political threat to American businessmen and landowners. In January 1893 a group of powerful Americans, supported by a contingent of U.S. Marines, overthrew the Hawaiian government and deposed the queen.

To save the lives of her people, Queen Lili'uokalani signed an official document, agreeing to give up her throne without further conflict. She was imprisoned in her own palace and tried for treason. Found guilty, she was sentenced to five years of hard labor, although the punishment was later reduced. On July 7, 1898, the U.S. Congress voted to annex Hawaii.

Results of Western Colonialism

Within sixty-six years the entire Pacific had been partitioned by seven major colonial powers. The Spanish were eventually forced out, leaving the countries of Germany, Great Britain, France, the Netherlands, Australia, and New Zealand to divide the spoils. The seventh country, the United States, joined the race to obtain colonies by annexing Hawaii and part of the Samoa Islands toward the end of the nineteenth century. An eighth country, Chile, maintained its presence on and control of Easter Island throughout this period.

European colonization stripped the Pacific Islanders of their land and its resources. Western governments also destroyed many traditional ways of life while forcing the indigenous people to live under unfamiliar forms of government and law.

Great ecological damage also was done to the landscape and ecology of many Pacific Islands. In Hawaii, for instance, sugarcane and pineapple, two crops that were introduced by Europeans and Americans, quickly crowded out many native herbs and vegetables. Logging operations caused the loss of thousands of acres of rain forest. Goats and cattle, also introduced by Western nations, ate huge amounts of plant life, often destroying acres of once productive farmland. Mongooses, brought in to control the rat population, instead of killing the rodents, feasted on bird eggs. This loss of so many eggs before measures were taken to protect bird nests played a significant role in causing the extinction of many native bird species. Similar environmental disasters occurred throughout the Pacific region.

The Early Years of the Twentieth Century

During the first half of the twentieth century the Western powers increased their control on most of the islands in the Pacific. Many colonies changed hands following the defeat of Germany in World War I. As a result of that defeat, Germany lost its colonial presence in the Pacific.

Throughout the region indigenous populations continued to diminish in

In 1891 Princess Lili'uokalani became queen of Hawaii. She was deposed two years later when the United States overthrew the Hawaiian monarchy.

size, while many facets of their traditional ways of life were lost forever. Missionaries continued to play a very active role as their efforts to Christianize the islanders intensified. European and American settlers continued to drift toward the islands and their numbers grew.

The colonial powers believed that the islanders were still totally unprepared to assume any role in government. Indeed, public opinion of the time held indigenous peoples everywhere to be backward and untrustworthy and, for the most part, lazy, careless, and irresponsible.

These opinions were magnified with the discovery of a "lost tribe" in New Guinea in the 1930s. Michael and Dan Leahy, two Australian prospectors, had happened upon some Papuans who were living a very primitive way of life. Michael Leahy recorded the following in his diary: "They were . . . thieving, godless, sneaky, cruel, murdering, disgusting, wicked, cruel, shiftless and immoral."[70]

Unfortunately Leahy's words were mirrored in the actions and beliefs of the majority of whites in the Pacific. Perfectly content to exert firm control over aspects of island culture that offended their tastes or threatened their property, the Europeans and Americans made little effort toward improving the indigenous peoples' lot in life. It would take the Second World War and the years that followed to provide the impetus for any change.

World War II

In late 1941 the Japanese began to sweep through the Pacific in hopes of establishing a base from which they could block the military shipping routes between the United States and Australia. By early 1942 the Japanese had captured port cities in New Guinea and the Solomon Islands. From there they hoped to prepare an assault on Australia.

Thousands of deaths resulted from the heavy fighting on these island groups. In New Guinea alone, over half a million soldiers from the two opposing sides eventually landed and fought for control of the island. Village life was completely disrupted, while the constant bombings by both sides took a high toll in lives.

On islands throughout the Pacific various indigenous groups supported the United States and the Allies in a myriad of different ways. Many natives joined in the fighting as active members of the armed forces of Australia, New Zealand, and the United States. Villagers also led brilliant guerrilla attacks that disrupted Japanese supply lines and the movement of Japanese soldiers. Others joined support groups and unloaded cargo, acted as scouts and spies, brought arms to the front lines, and helped with burials. Allied personnel were quick to show their appreciation of the islanders' sacrifices in support of the war effort, marking the first time since Westerners had colonized the Pacific that the local people were treated with respect.

Some of the heaviest fighting in the war took place on a small island in the Solomons called Guadalcanal. When the Japanese invaded Guadalcanal in March 1942, thousands of resident Europeans fled the island. Before they left, the Westerners burned

During an atomic weapons test in the Marshall Islands, the fallout from a nuclear explosion rains down on an island in the Pacific.

down everything they could, including the big plantations. Left nearly defenseless, the islanders faced the enemy alone. The Japanese swept through the island looting, stealing, torturing, and killing thousands of natives.

On August 6, 1942, American troops landed on Guadalcanal to begin a two-year campaign to rid the island of the Japanese. Over eighty thousand men from both sides battled through the small island, laying waste to huge areas of land. When the war ended the Japanese and Americans de-

parted, leaving the islanders with the debris of those years of destruction.

Atomic Testing in the Pacific

Following World War II the United States, Great Britain, and France began to use many of the Pacific Islands for extensive testing of atomic weapons. They justified these aerial bombardments as a way to gain nuclear supremacy over Communist Russia during the Cold War of the latter half of the twentieth century. Between 1946 and 1958 the United States exploded twenty-three bombs on the islands of Bikini and Eniwetok, while the French conducted over 150 tests on several islands in French Polynesia. The impact of these explosions on human, animal, and plant life is still being evaluated.

In June 1946 the U.S.Navy met with the 167 residents of the small island of Bikini in Micronesia. The islanders were a peaceful people who fished, hunted turtle eggs, built outrigger canoes, and ate coconuts. A navy representative explained to the islanders that the Americans needed their island for a project that, he said, would benefit all mankind. The officer went on to tell the people that they would need to leave their island homes for a short time but could soon return.

According to writer Louise B. Young, the chief, a man named Juda, replied, "If the United States government and the scientists of the world want to use our island and atoll for furthering development, which with God's blessing, will result in kindness and benefit to all mankind, my people will be pleased to go elsewhere."[71]

The entire population of Bikini Island along with their homes and belongings were moved to another island. "Unfortunately," writes Young, "this was just the beginning of a woeful saga. They became nomads of

A 1950 cartoon illustrates public defenselessness against nuclear attack.

the atomic age and were repeatedly relocated to other Pacific islands where they found only unhappiness."[72]

A huge blast named Bravo took place in 1954. This was the most powerful bomb ever exploded by the United States up to that time. Almost immediately it became apparent to American scientists that a serious mistake had been made.

The bomb was far more powerful than they had expected, and due to a sudden shift in the wind direction, radioactive ash fell on the naval vessels observing the test and on a Japanese fishing boat that had drifted close to the site. The members of the Japanese crew felt the effects of radiation poisoning almost immediately. By the third day many had fevers and their skin began to turn darker, while open sores developed on their fingers and exposed skin. One death and a number of illnesses resulted.

By 1978 it was determined that Bikini was so heavily impregnated with radioactive bomb debris that the island was not safe for human habitation. The same thing happened on Eniwetok Atoll and in French Polynesia. Although the United States stopped nuclear testing in the Pacific in 1963, France continued to detonate bombs well into the 1990s.

In early 2002 scientists and politicians admitted that the tests caused thousands of cancer-related deaths and illnesses not previously disclosed.

The Independence Movements

The respect that had been shown to the islanders by American and Allied troops during World War II and in the years that followed made a big impression on the natives. In addition, many islanders met African American soldiers and sailors who had some of the same privileges as their white compatriots. Seeing "free" people of their own skin color encouraged many native groups to look and work toward their own improvement and freedom.

U.S. Presence in Micronesia

There are more than three thousand islands in Micronesia, most of which are uninhabited. The main occupied islands are Yap, Chuuk, Pohnpei, and Kosrae. Some of these islands are so small that they fail to appear on maps of the world.

Many bitter battles were fought on these islands during World War II. Following the cessation of hostilities, most of Micronesia was placed under American control in a trusteeship arrangement set by the newly founded United Nations. The American military along with the Central Intelligence Agency kept several of the islands strictly off-limits to visitors for many decades and used some of the sites for nuclear testing and other classified operations.

Rather than allowing the indigenous residents to take over the government, the United States has maintained firm control over these islands. Micronesia in 2002 remains affiliated with United States and depends heavily on foreign aid and food imports to support and feed its population.

After World War II the appeal and need for colonies also greatly diminished. It became increasingly expensive to maintain colonies in faraway places. With world opinion changing, the United Nations criticized many nations for controlling and running native governments.

The civil rights movement of the 1960s in the United States also added fuel to the yearning for independence, and political activist groups were formed on many of the islands. As was true in Africa and other places, the people of the Pacific eventually benefited from this change in political and economic outlook.

By the 1990s nearly all the countries in the Pacific had gained some form of independence. Those that became fully independent include the nations of Kiribati, Nauru, Papua New Guinea, Western Samoa, Tuvalu, New Zealand, and Vanuatu. All now have democratically elected parliaments led by a prime minister. Hawaii became an American state in 1959. French Polynesia and New Caledonia send representatives to the French parliament but have yet to attain independence. Much of Micronesia still remains affiliated with the United States.

The island of Tonga gained full independence from Great Britain in 1970. An independence movement of a different kind has been taking place in Tonga, the only Pacific Island country still ruled by a monarch. Young Tongans, influenced by Western ideals, are now questioning the role of the monarchy. There is a growing movement on that island for a more democratic government.

The Call for Independence from France

France is one of the few countries not to relinquish its overseas territories in French Polynesia and New Caledonia. During the last few years of the twentieth century there has been an increased call, not only from the native people but also from world leaders, for independence from France. Most political experts, however, agree that it is unlikely this will happen in the near future.

Yvette Oopa is a descendant of one of Polynesia's heroes. In the 1950s she vocally opposed French dominion over the islands of French Polynesia. She was arrested and spent eight years in prison. Her words to writer Peter Benchley summed up the feelings of many Pacific indigenous people about their desire for independence. In the late 1990s she stated, "We are becoming foreigners in our own country. We're taught in school that our ancestors were [the French]. All we ask is to be permitted to be ourselves, live our lives, determine our own fate."[73]

After World War II the native Kanaks of New Caledonia began making more political demands on the French government. According to the *Lonely Planet's Guide*, Chief Naisseline led a local group in demanding more rights, arguing "that because Kanaks had fought and died under the French flag in both world wars, they were entitled to the rights of French citizens."[74] The Kanaks were finally granted citizenship in 1946 and the right to vote in 1957.

French Nuclear Testing

Long after the United States and other nations agreed to stop nuclear testing in the Pacific, the French continued to explode weapons in the region. A French test in September 1995 on the island of Moruroa set off a wave of violent riots and protests in many parts of French Polynesia. Over one thousand Tahitian natives took control of the capital city of Papeete's airport and then burned the building to the ground. Hundreds of demonstrators were arrested. The protesters continued to complain that France had long ignored their wishes and their rights. They also charged that the bombings were doing irreparable harm to the environment.

Numerous accidents and deaths have occurred in the region as a result of the nuclear tests. Barbara Deaver, editor of the *Cook Islands' Press,* reported on the aftermath of the explosion in an interview with Mel Kernahan.

Kernahan reports Deaver's comments in his article "South Sea Fallout," which appeared in the October 13, 1995, edition of *New Statesman and Society.*

Deaver reported, "Men sat blinking back tears as they heard a fellow Moruroa worker tell of how his five children died. . . . One man lifted his shirt and showed lesions on his chest." According to Kernahan, hundreds of people suffering from various health problems were taken to military hospitals in French Polynesia and Paris. Many came home in caskets.

In 1996 the French announced that there would be no further testing in the Pacific.

The Kanaks continued to actively call for independence. Riots broke out in the 1980s and chaos and violence persisted in New Caledonia during the next ten years. French paratroopers were ultimately flown in and a state of emergency was declared. The Noumea Accords, which restored peace to the area in 1998, were interpreted by Kanak activists as a blow to independence, since under the terms of the agreement independence could not come until 2013 at the earliest. Fear of additional violence was cited as the reason for the delay. In the view of the *Lonely Planet's Guide,* however, "It is more likely that France views New Caledonia as an economic and political asset it does not wish to lose."[75]

Tremendous changes have taken place on the islands of the Pacific in the last two hundred years. Bitterly oppressed by Western governments for many decades, many newly independent indigenous people are now attempting to regain control of their own lives and nations.

Chapter 7

Moving into the Twenty-First Century

As the indigenous people of the Pacific enter the twenty-first century, they face a myriad of problems. The islanders struggle with racism, unemployment, civil unrest, crime, poor health, and poverty. Many of the newly independent governments are also contending with political corruption, civil unrest, and economic uncertainty.

Despite these difficulties there is also a pervading sense of hope about the future. During the last forty years there has been a steady and growing interest in saving and reestablishing many of their ancient traditions. This movement has resulted in a cultural renaissance that today is impacting every facet of native society.

Village Life Today in the Pacific

Most Pacific Islanders still live in farming and fishing villages in the same kind of thatched-roofed dwellings their ancestors used. These villagers live off the land, relying on hunting, fishing, and subsistence

Two Papuan boys visit a market in Papua New Guinea, one of the least developed countries in the world.

farming to feed their families. While living conditions vary from island to island, poverty and under-education remain the norm.

This is particularly true on the Melanesian island of Papua New Guinea. According to journalist Jan Knippers Black, "By the usual standard of living indices, Papua New Guinea would have to be considered among the world's least developed countries."[76] With few roads into the interior, the Papuans, for the most part live isolated and traditional lives. It is estimated that around four out of five people in that country still live in rural communities and depend on subsistence agriculture for their livelihood.

And according to *National Geographic* journalist Francois Leydet, "The people in the bush . . . still carry on in the old ways. . . .

Most are where they were a hundred years ago."[77] To add credence to his statement, the journalist describes one of the villagers he met: "He was arrayed in traditional finery: feathered headdress, quill piercing the nose, peg-tooth necklace, loincloth."[78]

The majority of the indigenous people on the Solomon Islands also live in small villages of between one hundred and two hundred people. The same is true in Fiji, where many of the small villages are poverty-stricken. They have no running water and use communal toilets.

Even the most remote villages, however, have felt the effects of modern life. Nearly

Ecological Problems

Air pollution from modern industries has become a growing problem in many urban areas of the Pacific. Unfortunately, this is not the only ecological concern facing the area today.

Most of the islands are experiencing growing populations and acute land shortages. The natural resources on some of the islands are not sufficient to support these population increases. The island of Kiribati, for example, is so overpopulated that nearly five thousand people will be forced in the near future to move off that island to another location. Other islands, like the Cook Islands, have managed to keep this problem in check through voluntary immigration to other places.

The island of Tuvalu is experiencing a different kind of problem. This island is one of the lowest-lying nations in the world. The fear among scientists is that global warming could cause such massive flooding that the entire island could vanish beneath the sea.

Several of the French Polynesian islands are experiencing the effects of overexploitation of coral reefs and overfishing. Fishing, which has for a thousand years provided food and jobs, is under stress from modern fishing techniques. As a result, several fish populations are in danger of extinction. In addition, the reefs themselves have suffered extensive damage from careless accidents, pollutants, and temperature changes attributed to global warming.

every community has some form of store or market that sells processed or canned food items. A visitor would also see cars, trucks, bicycles, schools, health clinics, and even Western clothing in many of these communities.

Health Care

One of the biggest problems in rural areas is poor health. Village populations suffer from more health problems and have a much shorter life span than the nonindigenous people of the islands who live mainly in the cities. Malnutrition contributes to the health problems and plays a significant role in the high mortality rates among children. Inadequate sanitation in rural areas also leads to high rates of disease, particularly malaria and intestinal infections. To make matters worse, health care services are not readily available in many remote and isolated areas of the Pacific.

To combat these persistent problems most island governments are now spending more money on health care. Teams of doctors and nurses fly to many remote villages and provide basic health care services. With the help of the United Nations and the World Health Organization, stronger efforts also are being made to combat malaria by educating the na-

tives and reducing the mosquito populations.

Health education is particularly important in Papua New Guinea where health statistics are the worst of any island nation. Leydet describes a unique method of teach-

Even today, a Pacific Islands villager displays the traditional headdress and bone piercing.

Political Unrest in Fiji

One of the greatest challenges facing Fiji today is political instability. The problem originated over one hundred years ago when Great Britain, looking for cheap labor, brought over thousands of workers from East India to harvest the sugarcane. Many Indians stayed, and by the end of the twentieth century, represented half the Fijian population. While the Fijians maintained control over the land, the Indians gradually worked their way into important positions in business and politics.

In 1987, for the first time, the Indian Party won the country's elections. The Fijians, concerned about what would happen to their land holdings, staged a military coup and overthrew the government. Proclaiming that Fiji should be controlled and run by native Fijians, the revolutionaries instituted a new constitution that took away many of the Indians' rights.

The country's political situation never really quieted down after that. As the Indians gradually regained some of their rights and Fiji elected its first prime minister of Indian descent, Mahendra Chaudry, more trouble erupted. Chaudry's election in 1999 was viewed as another threat by native Fijians.

Led by George Speight, a militant Fijian nationalist, a private army stormed the government's buildings in May 2000 and took Chaudry and thirty members of his parliament hostage. Speight called for a new constitution that would return power to the Fijians. Riots, arson, and violence erupted in the cities. Eventually, international outrage led to Speight's arrest. The militant awaits trial, while the political unrest in Fiji continues.

ing preventive health care in that country. Leydet writes, "Actors with masks representing a dog, a pig and a fly conveyed the message that allowing animals inside the huts causes [disease] in humans."[79] This theatrical troupe, called the Raun Raun Theater, also performs skits about other health problems, including the need for birth control. Such efforts emphasizing preventive health care have dramatically decreased the number of deaths among mothers and their infants in New Guinea.

Urban Life

During the latter years of the twentieth century thousands of Pacific Islanders moved to various cities and towns in search of employment and better living conditions. Many of those individuals ended up in migrant settlements on the outskirts of urban areas. In Suva, the capital city of Fiji, for instance, over five thousand indigenous families are classified as squatters and reside in tenement-like structures.

Foreign visitors to the Pacific Islands rave about a tropical paradise with strikingly beautiful scenery. Rarely, however, do they see a true picture of native life. Tourists usually do not see the poor who sleep on the streets; they are not aware of the hunger strikers; and they seldom are shown the soldiers and the barbed wire enclosures that surround many resorts. According to journalist Mel Kernahan, "Slum housing made of discarded junk sprawls for miles outside [Papeete, the capital city of Tahiti]. . . . Too many [natives], who once had land that grew everything necessary to support human existence, are now, literally dirt poor."[80]

Many Hawaiian natives have a problem of a different kind. It is now very expensive to live on their islands. Throughout the archipelago there has been a tremendous growth in construction during the last thirty years. Resorts and golf courses have expanded into previously natural environments and have encroached on traditional native land. As land prices increased, only the very wealthy have been able to buy land. As a result, many descendants of independent farmers, fishermen, and artisans now live in villages, welfare housing, or even tenements.

Modern Urban Problems

Urban crime has become a significant problem for many island societies. Gangs of unemployed native youth have turned many towns and urban areas into violent places. Youth gangs with names like the Mongrel Mob roam the streets of Auckland, New Zealand, while in Papua New Guinea gangs of unemployed native boys,

The Ironman Triathlon is a yearly event on the big island of Hawaii. In the grueling race, competitors from all over the world swim, bike, and run a total of 141 miles.

called "rascals," have brought fear and violence to many towns and urban areas.

Alcoholism and drug addiction also pose problems for the native populations of the Pacific. As is true in many other indigenous societies, the abuse of these substances stems in part from the loss of traditional values. Facing unemployment, poverty, and homelessness, many turn to alcohol and drugs to ease their pain and frustration.

On the island of Fiji even the traditional use of kava has become a problem. While kava does not cause drunkenness, it is a mild narcotic. Its effects range from light-headedness to a false sense of euphoria, often causing drastic reductions in the quality and quantity of work, which in turn produce problems for businesses.

Most sociologists agree that without the traditional support of their families and communities, many young people have no anchor in life and turn to drugs, crime, and alcohol as an outlet for their frustrations. Political activist and Maori leader Tom Fox agrees with this assertion. In a 1984 interview with journalists Yva Momatiuk and John Eastcott, Fox stated, "You know many of our youngsters get in trouble in the cities. They have lost their *maoritanga*—the Maori pride and sense of belonging."[81]

The Effects of Racism

A contributing factor to the many problems facing the indigenous people is racism. According to Hawaiian Phil Kwiatkowski, "Even when I was growing up [in the 1950s and 1960s], Hawaiians were considered second-class citizens. To be Hawaiian carried a certain stigma—it meant you were ignorant, lazy, primitive, pagan."[82]

A man drinks kava during a ceremony in Fiji. Kava is a mildly narcotic beverage made from the roots of the kava plant.

Indeed, despite many improvements in their standard of living during the latter years of the twentieth century, the indigenous people of the Pacific still contend with problems caused by racism. Journalist Peter Benchley describes the situation for the French Polynesians: "What is at issue is the . . . unanimously held perception . . . that they are treated as second-class citizens in their own land, that in everything from jobs to . . . income, French people are given preference over Polynesians."[83]

At the end of the twentieth century Hawaiian statistics showed that native Polynesians made up less than 20 percent of the population. In spite of these low numbers, native Hawaiians make up half of the state's prison inmates and half of the homeless. In addition, their health is ranked the worst of any group in the United States. New Zealand journalist Geoff Lealand summarizes: "They remain short-changed, being over-represented among the impoverished, the unemployed, and the imprisoned."[84]

Unrest and Rebellion in Papua New Guinea

Another significant problem in the Pacific is political corruption and civil strife. On many islands these problems have led to rebellions and outbreaks of violence.

One of the most serious conflicts occurred on the island of Bougainville in Papua New Guinea. In the 1960s huge amounts of copper were discovered on Bougainville, followed in 1969 by the establishment of the Panguna Mine under the management of an Australian company. When this new mine opened, thousands of Bougainville residents were evicted from their land.

In 1988 the tensions escalated as natives demanded their share of the immense profits being made at the mine. They were also angered that hundreds of acres of land were being destroyed because of the mining process. These complaints led to the formation of the Bougainville Revolutionary Army, whose rebels successfully closed down what was at the time the world's most profitable copper mine.

The government of Papua New Guinea, with the support of the Australians, sent in riot police and the military in an effort to reopen the mine. According to journalist Jan Knippers Black, "[Violent acts by both sides] have claimed about twenty thousand lives and allegedly resulted in summary execution, disappearances and tortures on the part of the Papua New Guinea defense forces."[85]

In 1996 an Inter-Church Women's Forum was called by seven hundred Bougainville women to talk about how to end the conflict. According to journalist Conception Garcia Ramilo, "The Forum brought to the surface a long list of human rights abuses against women in the ongoing war. . . . Women were being interrogated, arrested, raped and even murdered. Villages were being looted, burned and sprayed with chemicals that kill animals and plants."[86]

The war in Bougainville officially ended in April 1998. Tensions smoldered

A classroom of students in Fiji, where the availability of higher education has increased in recent years.

in 2002 while the cease-fire was being monitored by a peacekeeping force from the United Nations.

Education and the Resurgence of Native Languages

Despite the existence of other conflicts in the Pacific, and despite the many problems still facing the native populations, there have been advances made in several areas. The increasing availability of education is one such area. Today, for example, all Pacific Island countries provide mandatory and free education for at least six years.

Only Fiji, Papua New Guinea, Guam, Western Samoa, New Zealand, and Hawaii, however, have any kind of vocational colleges or universities. The University of the South Pacific, located in Fiji, also offers many college courses via a satellite network. Attendance at these schools of higher learning has increased somewhat in recent years, producing a slowly growing number of native lawyers, physicians, and businesspeople.

The Maori of New Zealand, in particular, have seen a dramatic improvement in the percentage of natives who attend schools of higher learning. They now

Dame Kiri Te Kanawa

The Pacific Islands are home to hundreds of indigenous artists, performers, and craftsmen. One of the best known is world-renowned Maori opera star, Dame Kiri Te Kanawa. Growing up in a traditional native village on the island of New Zealand, Kiri (whose name means "bell" in Maori) used a grant from a native arts council to study singing in London.

In 1997 she sang at one of the world's greatest opera houses—the Royal Opera House in London's Covent Gardens. Since that time she has had the privilege of singing at the wedding of Prince Charles and Lady Diana in 1981.

Dame Kiri celebrated her native roots in the 1999 album *Maori Songs*, and many of her performances are shown on television in New Zealand, where she remains a source of great pride to her Maori kinsfolk.

Maori opera star Dame Kiri Te Kanawa (second from right) bows with costars after a performance in New York City.

have their own university, whose graduates hold many important positions in government, industry, and other professions. Several Maori also have been elected to the New Zealand House of Representatives.

Few islanders, however, can afford this kind of higher education, and most quit school when they reach the ages of twelve to fourteen. This is especially true in Papua New Guinea where few villagers go beyond the six-year limit. This also is the case in the Solomons, where the literacy rate is less than 50 percent.

This lack of education contributes to high native unemployment rates on many islands. Most islanders end up in low-paying manual labor positions which offer little opportunity for advancement. Despite recent advancements in the availability of education, the majority of indigenous people in the Pacific remain under-educated.

One area of hope and perhaps the greatest recent accomplishment in the realm of education has been the reintroduction of native language in school curricula. Throughout the Pacific proud inheritors of indigenous cultures continue to work diligently to save their traditional languages, many of which were nearly eradicated when the missionaries arrived. In many places children are now taught these languages in school, while interested adults can attend night language courses. In addition, numerous native groups who are in danger of losing their myths and stories are making an effort to write down these tales for future generations.

Resurgence of Traditional Arts and Culture

There also has been a tremendous resurgence of traditional art and culture among the indigenous people of the Pacific during the last forty years. Many ancient practices once again are being followed openly, while thousands of islanders have turned back to many of the crafts of long ago.

Descendants of the statue makers of Easter Island, for instance, once again are making their own art and have reinstituted the ancient art of tattooing. Hundreds of Rapa Nui are also performing their traditional music and dance. The Kari Kari Company performs native chants and dancing. According to Jimmy Araki, one of the musicians, "We're trying to keep the culture alive. We're trying to recuperate all our ancient stuff and put it back together and give it a new uprising."[87]

Other islanders elsewhere have rediscovered the art of canoe building. In New Zealand the Maori hold an annual competition during which traditional canoes are raced. Held on the Waikato River on North Island, teams compete against each other in elaborately decorated war canoes.

In Hawaii work on the restoration of many historic and sacred sites is being stepped up. The Polynesian Cultural Center was built on the island of Oahu in the late 1960s in order to celebrate the various Pacific cultures. Seven different villages have been recreated: Hawaiian, Tongan, Samoan, Fijian, Tahitian, Maori, and Marquesan. Natives from each of the island groups act as guides.

Learning a Lesson from the Past

Many of the island countries in the Pacific presently face the problems of overpopulation and the loss of natural resources. Isolated from other land masses, most island nations, despite trade with other countries, are still largely dependent on the resources of their own islands. The indigenous people of Easter Island learned the hard way what happens when resources are eradicated.

When the first people arrived on Easter Island over a thousand years ago, the land looked very different than it does today. The island was covered with thick forests and palm trees. By the time the Europeans arrived in the eighteenth century, however, the land was barren and desolate, covered only with rocks.

Easter Island culture flourished for over six hundred years. Sweet potatoes, bananas, and yams were cultivated, canoes were built, and trees were cut down to build fine houses. In the seventeenth century, however, conflict and warfare on the island increased and the indigenous society began to disintegrate. Timber became scarce, while the soil deteriorated due to constant cultivation. Crops failed, and without the forests there was no wood to build canoes. Unable to leave the island, the people suffered. By the time the Europeans arrived the population was only a fraction of what it had been at its peak.

The Suva Hibiscus Festival, started in Fiji in 1956, lasts over a week during August. It brings together cultural performances by many different native groups. Among the events that take place are a beauty pageant, a fashion show, food tasting, music, games, and dancing. The Maori have a similar festival called the Aotearoa Traditional Arts Festival.

Today many islanders are bicultural, leading a Western lifestyle but still following many of the ancient ways of life. This is particularly true for the Maori of New Zealand. It is not unusual, for example, for a Maori man to work all week in an office speaking English and then spend the weekend in a spirit house, or *marae,* where only Maori is spoken. It is estimated that there are over one thousand of these ceremonial gathering places still in existence, many of which are now used as schools for carving, weaving, and other traditional arts.

Hope for the Future

As the indigenous people of the Pacific enter the twenty-first century, many are for the first time taking an active role in politics and industry. The Maori, for instance, have been very active during the last twenty years in demanding greater access to services and the rights to their former land holdings. As a result of this activism, many important lands and fishing rights were returned to the natives in the late 1980s. And in 1995 Queen Elizabeth II of Great Britain offered a formal apology to the Maori for the many treaty violations of the past.

Natives on Easter Island have not been so fortunate, but they are beginning to see some progress. Easter Island is still governed by Chile, but according to Paul Trachtman, "Under growing pressures, the Chilean government is giving back a small number of homesteads to native families."[88]

Tourism, Industry, and Native Pride

Many indigenous peoples are now benefiting from tourism, the number-one industry throughout the Pacific. On the positive side, tourism has stimulated the building of roads, airports, shops, hotels, restaurants, and resorts—all of which have provided many employment opportunities for the indigenous people. And yet even tourism has its negative effects. According to writer Jan Morris,

> Hawaiian civilization has been debased by generations of occupation and tourism. Its ancient music has been vulgarized. Its ritual dances have been trivialized. Its language has been ignorantly plundered or patronized as a tourist gimmick. Half-submerged, the culture does live on—passionate enthusiasts keep the language going, and, at almost any of the old Hawaiian temples, dedicated to the gods of long ago, you may still see offerings of flowers and fruit.[89]

Indigenous populations are also beginning to profit from other island industries.

In French Polynesia, for instance, there is a relatively new and growing industry based around the seeding, growing, harvesting, exporting, and retailing of black pearls. The export of copra, pineapple, and sugarcane is also bringing profits to many island nations.

After two hundred years of oppression the indigenous people of the Pacific are once again controlling many aspects of their own lives. Native pride and adaptability enabled the natives to survive the years of Western domination. The same factors are now playing a significant role in the resurgence of native cultures. While there are still many problems to overcome, the people of the Pacific can look to the future with hope.

Notes

Introduction: Isolated Lands

1. National Geographic Books, eds. *Mysteries of Mankind*. Washington, DC: National Geographic Books, 1992, p. 74.
2. David Howarth, *Tahiti: A Paradise Lost*. New York: Viking, 1983, p. 26.

Chapter One: The Great Migration

3. Robert C. Kiste, "Oceania: Overview," *Countries of the World*, January 1, 1991, n.p.
4. Goran Burenhult, *New World and Pacific Civilizations*. San Francisco: Harper, 1994, p. 162.
5. Simon Robinson, "South Pacific: History in Their Blood DNA," *Time International*, September 7, 1998, n.p.
6. Burenhult, *New World and Pacific Civilizations*, p. 164.
7. Time-Life Books, eds., *Southeast Asia: A Past Regained*. Alexandria, VA: Time-Life Books, 1995, p. 15.
8. Burenhult, *New World and Pacific Civilizations*, p. 149.
9. David Kawaharada, "The Settlement of Polynesia," Part I, *Polynesian Voyaging Society*. www.kcc.hawaii.edu.
10. Frans Lanting and Christine K. Eckstrom, *Forgotten Edens*. Washington, DC: National Geographic Books, 1993, p. 103.
11. Kawaharada, "The Settlement of Polynesia, Part I."

12. Reader's Digest, eds., *Everyday Life Throughout the Ages*. London: Reader's Digest Association, 1992, p. 327.
13. Burenhult, *New World and Pacific Civilizations*, p. 156.

Chapter Two: Everyday Life in the Pacific

14. Bill Strubbe, "In the Wake of Captain Cook," *The World and I*. July 1, 2000, n.p.
15. Edward Marriott, *The Lost Tribe*. New York: Henry Holt, 1996, p. 150.
16. Roger Vaughan, "The Two Worlds of Fiji," *National Geographic,* October 1995, p. 122.
17. National Geographic Books, eds., Mysteries of Mankind, p. 181.
18. *Lonely Planet's Guide*, "New Caledonia: History and Culture." http://aolsvc.travel/aol.com.
19. Moana Tregaskis, *Hawaii*. Oakland, CA: Fodor's Travel Publications, 1988, p. 43.
20. Tregaskis, *Hawaii*, p. 43.
21. National Geographic Books, eds., *Mysteries of Mankind*, p. 76.
22. Douglas Newton, "Maoris: Treasures of the Tradition," *National Geographic*, October 1984, p. 542.

Chapter Three: Island Communities and Families

23. "Lords of the Dance," *Culture of the Cook Islands*. www.ck/culture.htm

24. Robert C. Kiste, "Oceania: Traditional Societies," *Countries of the World*, January 1, 1991, n.p.

25. Reader's Digest, eds., *Everyday Life Throughout the Ages*, p. 334.

26. Tony Wheeler, Nancy Keller, and Jeff Williams, *New Zealand*. Victoria, Australia: Lonely Planet, 1994, p. 14.

27. Wheeler et al, *New Zealand*, p. 16.

28. *Lonely Planet's Guide*, "French Polynesia: History and Culture." http://aolsvc.travel/aol.com.

29. Paul Theroux, *The Happy Isles of Oceania*. New York: Ballentine Books, 1992, p. 333.

30. Margaret Mead, *Coming of Age in Samoa*. New York: William Morrow, 1961, p. 33.

31. Jean-Michel Cousteau and Mose Richards, *Cousteau's Papua New Guinea Journey*. New York: Harry N. Abrams, 1989, p. 96.

32. Mead, *Coming of Age in Samoa*, p. 16.

33. Mead, *Coming of Age in Samoa*, p. 16.

34. *Lonely Planet's Guide*, "American Samoa: History and Culture," http://aolsvc.travel/aol.com.

35. National Geographic Books, eds., *Primitive Worlds: People Lost in Time*. Washington, DC: National Geographic Books, 1973, p. 81.

36. Quoted in National Geographic Books, eds., *Primitive Worlds*, p. 67.

Chapter Four: Religion and Magic

37. *Lonely Planet's Guide*, "Vanuatu: History and Culture." http://aolsvc.travel/aol.com.

38. Quoted in Theroux, *The Happy Isles of Oceania*, p. 179.

39. Howarth, *Tahiti*, p. 27.

40. Burenhult, *New World and Pacific Civilizations*, p. 172.

41. Wheeler et al, *New Zealand*, p. 13.

42. National Geographic Books, eds., *Primitive Worlds*, p. 65.

43. Reader's Digest, eds., *Everyday Life Throughout the Ages*, p. 327.

44. Kiste, "Oceania: Traditional Societies," n.p.

45. Tim Cahill, *Pass the Butterworms*. New York: Vintage Books, 1997, p. 267.

46. Shirley Nicholson, ed., *Shamanism*. Wheaton, Illinois: Theosophical Publishing House, 1987, p. 190.

47. Wheeler et al, *New Zealand*, p. 13.

48. Mead, *Coming of Age in Samoa*, p. 93.

49. Cahill, *Pass the Butterworms*, p. 263.

50. Marriott, *The Lost Tribe*, p. 25.

51. Cahill, *Pass the Butterworms*, p. 266.

52. Burenhult, *New World and Pacific Civilizations*, p. 172.

53. Francois Leydet, "Papua New Guinea: Journey Through Time," *National Geographic*, August 1982, p. 166.

54. Quoted in Paul Trachtman, "Mysterious Island," *Smithsonian Magazine*, March 2002, p. 92.

Chapter Five: The Rediscovery of the Pacific Islands

55. Robert C. Kiste, "Oceania: Era of Discovery," *Countries of the World*, January 1, 1991, n.p.

56. Quoted in Ruth M. Tabrah, *Hawaii: A History*. New York: W. W. Norton, 1980, p. 16.

57. Quoted in Tregaskis, *Hawaii*, p. 26.
58. Cousteau and Richards, *Cousteau's Papua New Guinea Journey*, p. 66.
59. Reader's Digest Books, eds., *Everyday Life Throughout the Ages*, p. 327.
60. Kiste, "Oceania: Era of Discovery," n.p.
61. Wheeler, *New Zealand*, p. 16.
62. Marriott, *The Lost Tribe*, p. 12.
63. Marriott, *The Lost Tribe*, p. 182.
64. Quoted in Cynthia Russ Ramsay, *Hawaii's Hidden Treasures*. Washington, DC: National Geographic Books, 1993 p. 123.
65. Kiste, "Oceania: Era of Discovery," n.p.

Chapter Six: From Colonialism to Independence
66. Tabrah, *Hawaii*, p. 23.
67. Wheeler et al, *New Zealand*, p. 18.
68. Donald Seekins, "New Caledonia: General Information." *Countries of the World*, January 1, 1991, n.p.
69. *Lonely Planet's Guide*, "Kiribati: History and Culture." http://aolsvc.travel/aol.com.
70. Quoted in Marriott, *The Lost Tribe*, p. 95.
71. Quoted in Louise B. Young, *Islands*. New York: W. H. Freeman, 1994, p. 208.
72. Young, *Islands*, p. 208.
73. Quoted in Peter Benchley, "Charting a New Course: French Polynesia," *National Geographic*, June 1997, p. 14.
74. *Lonely Planet's Guide*, "New Caledonia."
75. *Lonely Planet's Guide*, "New Caledonia."

Chapter Seven: Moving into the Twenty-First Century
76. Jan Knippers Black, "Modern Materialism Catches Up with Papua New Guinea," *USA Today*, November 1, 1997.
77. Leydet, "Papua New Guinea," p. 155.
78. Leydet, "Papua New Guinea," p. 154.
79. Leydet, "Papua New Guinea," p. 154.
80. Mel Kernahan, "South Sea Fallout," *New Statesman and Society*, October 13, 1995, n.p.
81. Quoted in Yva Momatiuk and John Eastcott, "Maoris: Home in Two Worlds," *National Geographic*, October, 1984, p. 530.
82. Quoted in Louise E. Levathes, "Kamehameha," *National Geographic*, November 1983, p. 566.
83. Benchley, "Charting a New Course," p. 19.
84. Geoff Lealand, "American Popular Culture and Emerging Nationalism in New Zealand," *National Forum*, September 1, 1994, n.p.
85. Black, "Modern Materialism Catches Up with Papua New Guinea," n.p.
86. Conception Garcia Ramilo, "Breakthrough at Bougainville," *Contemporary Women's Issues Database*, January 3, 1997, n.p.
87. Quoted in Trachtman, "Mysterious Island," p. 98.

Epilogue: Hope for the Future
88. Trachtman, "Mysterious Island," p. 97.
89. Jan Morris, "Paradox in the Sun," *Travel Holiday,* October 1990, n.p.

For Further Reading

Books

Caroline Arnold, *Easter Island.* New York: Clarion Books, 2000. An excellent look at Easter Island, its settlement, and history.

Kate Darian-Smith, *Australia and Oceania.* Austin, TX: Raintree Steck-Vaughn, 1997. This excellent book looks at the peoples of Australia and the various islands of the Pacific Ocean.

Judith Diamond, *Solomon Islands.* Chicago: Childrens Press, 1995. The author presents an excellent glimpse of the Solomon Islands, its history, and its people.

Ayesha Ercelawn, *New Zealand.* Milwaukee, WI: Gareth Stevens, 2001. An excellent book about the country of New Zealand and its people.

Mary Virginia Fox, *Papua New Guinea.* Chicago: Childrens Press, 1994. This book offers a good look at the country of Papua New Guinea, its history, and its indigenous peoples.

Martin Hintz, *Hawaii.* Chicago: Childrens Press, 1999. An excellent look at Hawaii, its history, and its people.

Valerie Keyworth, *New Zealand.* Minneapolis: Dillon, 1990. An excellent book about New Zealand, its history, and its people.

Sharon Linnea, *Princess Ka'iulani.* Grand Rapids, MI: Eerdman Books, 1999. A look at the last years of the Hawaiian monarchy through the eyes of the young royal princess who was the next in line for the throne.

Barbara A. Margolies, *Warriors, Wigmen and the Crocodile People.* New York: Four Winds, 1993. The author looks at three different tribes of indigenous people in Papua New Guinea.

Roseline NgCheong-Lum, *Fiji.* New York: Marshall Cavendish, 2000. This excellent book looks at the island of Fiji and its people.

Fran Sammis, *Australia and the South Pacific.* New York: Marshall Cavendish, 2000. This book presents a basic look at Australia and the Pacific Islands.

Fay Stanley, *The Last Princess*. New York: Four Winds, 1991. A detailed account of the last years of Hawaii's monarchy and the rise of American interests which led to an overthrow of the native government.

Rafael Tilton, *The Importance of Margaret Mead*. San Diego: Lucent Books, 1994. An excellent book about the life of world-renowned anthropologist Margaret Mead, whose studies of the people of Samoa and New Guinea, among others, led to a greater understanding of indigenous cultures.

Edra Ziesk, *Margaret Mead*. New York: Chelsea House, 1990. An excellent look at the life and studies of anthropologist Margaret Mead.

Website

Lonely Planet's Guide (http://adsvc.travel/aol.com). This website provides a rich source of information about the peoples, culture, and history of the Pacific Islands.

Works Consulted

Books

Goran Burenhult, *New World and Pacific Civilizations*. San Francisco: Harper, 1994. An excellent book that focuses on many different cultures including those of the Melanesians, Polynesians, and Micronesians.

Tim Cahill, *Pass the Butterworms*. New York: Vintage Books, 1997. This book by a writer for *Outside* magazine offers a short chapter about the Karowai, a group of native people living in New Guinea.

Rick and Marcie Carroll, eds., *Hawaii: True Stories of the Island Spirit*. San Francisco: Travelers' Tales, 1999. This book offers a compilation of stories and essays about various aspects of Hawaii.

Jean-Michel Cousteau and Mose Richards, *Cousteau's Papua New Guinea Journey*. New York: Harry N. Abrams, 1989. An account of the *Calypso*'s voyage to New Guinea, where the crew had many interactions with different native tribes. A fascinating account, filled with pictures and interviews with natives.

Thor Heyerdahl, *Early Man and the Ocean*. New York: Doubleday, 1979. A detailed book by the world-renowned explorer and author tracing the development of sailing vessels and early oceanic exploration and discoveries.

———, *Easter Island*. New York: Random House, 1989. The famous explorer focuses on his theory that Easter Island and other Pacific Island countries were settled not by Polynesians but by ancient Incas from Peru.

Jean Howard, *Margaret Mead*. New York: Simon and Schuster, 1984. A biography of noted anthropologist and humanitarian Margaret Mead, whose work in Samoa and New Guinea, among other places, led to a greater understanding of indigenous society and culture.

David Howarth, *Tahiti: A Paradise Lost*. New York: Viking, 1983. An excellent look at the "discovery" of Tahiti by European explorers. The book offers a great deal of information about Tahiti in the eighteenth and nineteenth centuries.

Kelly Knauer, ed., *Great Discoveries*. New York: Time-Life Books, 2001. This book looks at the great discoveries of the twentieth century. One brief section looks at the movements and migrations of the Polynesians.

Frans Lanting and Christine K. Eckstrom, *Forgotten Edens*. Washington, DC: National Geographic Books, 1993. A look at many remarkable lands; includes a section on Hawaii and the Polynesians who settled there.

Edward Marriott, *The Lost Tribe*. New York: Henry Holt, 1996. The extraordinary story of a British journalist who journeys into the jungles of Papua New Guinea to live with the so-called "lost tribe" of the Liawep.

Margaret Mead, *Coming of Age in Samoa*. New York: William Morrow, 1961. Originally published in 1928, this book by well-known anthropologist Margaret Mead describes her extraordinary stay with the indigenous people of Samoa. While some of her conclusions are no longer accepted, Mead's work was ground-breaking at the time.

National Geographic Books, eds., *Mysteries of Mankind*. Washington, DC: National Geographic Books, 1992. A fascinating look at many of the world's mysteries, including a section on Easter Island and the stone temples of Nan Madol in Micronesia.

———, *Mysteries of the Ancient World*. Washington, DC: National Geographic Books, 1979. This book takes a close look at some of the many enduring mysteries of the world, including the stone statues of Easter Island.

———, *Primitive Worlds: People Lost in Time*. Washington, DC: National Geographic Books, 1973. A remarkable look at the Tifalmin tribe of Papua New Guinea, and the Mbotgate people of Malekula Island.

Shirley Nicholson, ed., *Shamanism*. Wheaton, IL: Theosophical Publishing House, 1987. This book is a compilation of essays about shamanism. There is an excellent section on Hawaiian shamanism and the kahuna cult.

Cynthia Russ Ramsay, *Hawaii's Hidden Treasures*. Washington, DC: National Geographic Books, 1993. While dealing primarily with the natural beauty and history of Hawaii, this book also looks at the indigenous people and some of their beliefs and ways of life.

Reader's Digest, eds., *Everyday Life Throughout the Ages*. London: Reader's Digest Association, 1992. A good resource book about the everyday life of numerous cultures, including that of the Maoris of New Zealand and the early Micronesians and Polynesians.

Ruth M. Tabrah, *Hawaii: A History*. New York: W. W. Norton, 1980. An older but excellent history of the Hawaiian Islands from their beginnings up to the 1970s. There are good sections on the indigenous Polynesian and early European explorers, especially Captain James Cook.

Paul Theroux, *The Happy Isles of Oceania*. New York: Ballentine Books, 1992. Well-known author Paul Theroux recounts his adventures as he travels by sea throughout the many islands of the Pacific. He focuses on many different cultures including the Melanesians, Micronesians, and Polynesians as he talks with the indigenous peoples of many countries.

Time-Life Books, eds., *Southeast Asia: A Past Regained*. Alexandria, VA. Time-Life Books, 1995. An interesting book about the rich traditions of Southeast Asia, with a good section about the seafarers and explorers who discovered many Pacific islands and settled there.

Moana Tregaskis, *Hawaii*. Oakland, CA: Fodor's Travel Publications, 1988. This predominantly travel-oriented book also offers a good deal of information about the history of Hawaii and the Polynesians.

Jennifer Westwood, *Mysterious Places*. New York: Barnes and Noble, 1987. The author looks at sacred sites, symbolic landscapes, ancient cities, and lost lands. There is a good section on Easter Island and its people.

Tony Wheeler, Nancy Keller, and Jeff Williams, *New Zealand*. Victoria, Australia: Lonely Planet, 1994. While this book focuses primarily on travel, it does present a good section on the history and peoples of New Zealand.

Louise B. Young, *Islands*. New York: W.H. Freeman, 1994. While focusing primarily on ecological issues, this book also looks at the history of many different islands including the Hawaiian archipelago, Easter Island, and some of the inhabited coral atolls of Polynesia and Micronesia.

Periodicals

Peter Benchley, "Charting a New Course: French Polynesia," *National Geographic*, June 1997.

Jan Knippers Black, "Modern Materialism Catches Up with Papua New Guinea," *USA Today*, November 1, 1997.

Shannon Brownlee, "Taking Back the Island," *U.S. News and World Report*, September 16, 1996.

Frederica M. Bunge, "Kiribati: General Information," *Countries of the World*, January 1, 1991.

———, "Western Samoa: General Information," *Countries of the World*, January 1, 1991.

Jane Clancy, "Hawaiian Legacy," *Colonial Home*, August 1, 1994.

Melinda W. Cooke, "Easter Island: General Information," *Countries of the World*, January 1, 1991.

Economist, "Fiji: The Trouble Ahead," June 3, 2000.

Ann Gibbons, "The People of the Pacific," *Science*, March 2, 2001.

Robert J. Gordon, "Papua New Guinea: Nation in the Making," *National Geographic*, August 1982.

Mel Kernahan, "South Sea Fallout," *New Statesman and Society*, October 13, 1995.

Robert C. Kiste, "Oceania: Era of Discovery," *Countries of the World*, January 1, 1991.

———, "Oceania: Overview," *Countries of the World*, January 1, 1991.

————, "Oceania: Traditional Societies," *Countries of the World,* January 1, 1991.

Stanley Krippner, Ann Mortifee, and David Feinstein, "New Myths for the New Millennium," *The Futurist*, March 1, 1998.

Geoff Lealand, "American Popular Culture and Emerging Nationalism in New Zealand," *National Forum*, September 1, 1994.

Louise E. Levathes, "Kamehameha," *National Geographic*, November 1983.

Francois Leydet, "Papua New Guinea: Journey Through Time," *National Geographic*, August 1982.

Yva Momatiuk and John Eastcott, "Maoris: Home in Two Worlds," *National Geographic*, October 1984.

Jane Monahan, "Bang Went All the Old Grass Skirt Cliches," *Independent on Sunday*, November 25, 2001.

Jan Morris, "Paradox in the Sun," *Travel Holiday*, October 1990.

Douglas Newton, "Maoris: Treasures of the Tradition," *National Geographic*, October 1984.

Conception Garcia Ramilo, "Breakthrough at Bougainville," *Contemporary Women's Issues Database*, January 3, 1997.

Simon Robinson, "South Pacific: History in Their Blood DNA," *Time International*, September 7, 1998.

Donald Seekins, "French Polynesia: General Information," *Countries of the World*, January 1, 1991.

————, "New Caledonia: General Information," *Countries of the World*, January 1, 1991.

Rinn-Sup Shinn, "Micronesia: Trust Territory," *Countries of the World*, January 1, 1991.

Bill Strubbe, "In the Wake of Captain Cook," *The World and I*, July 1, 2000.

Paul Trachtman, "Mysterious Island," *Smithsonian Magazine*, March 2002.

Hannah Tunnah, "Will Fiji Honor Election Result?" *Waikato Times*, August 28, 2001.

Roger Vaughan, "The Two Worlds of Fiji," *National Geographic*, October 1995.

George Wehrfritz, "Rebels of the Pacific," *Newsweek International*, August 16, 1999.

Stephan B. Wickman, "Tonga: General Information," *Countries of the World*, January 1, 1991.

David N. Zurick, "Preserving Paradise," *Geographical Review*, April 1, 1995.

Internet Sources

Ancient Polynesians, "Ancient Polynesians Settle in Hawaii." http://home.earthlink.net.

Bougainville Freedom Movement, "Bougainville Fights for Freedom." www.hartford-hwp.com.

Culture of the Cook Islands, "Lords of the Dance." www.ck/culture.htm.

Easter Island Homepage, "Rapa Nui." www.netaxs.com.

Fiji Government, "Europeans and the Twentieth Century." www.fiji.gov.

———, "History and Culture." www.fiji.gov.

Steven Roger Fischer, "Easter Island's Rongorongo Script," *Rongorongo by Steven Fischer*. www.netaxs.com

Hawaii—Independent and Sovereign, "Hawaiian Power." www.hawaii-nation.org.

History of the Cook Islands, "What Is Our Past?" www.ck/history.htm.

David Kawaharada, "The Settlement of Polynesia, Part I," *Polynesian Voyaging Society*. http://leahi.kcc.hawaii/edu/org.

Lonely Planet's Guide, "American Samoa: History and Culture." http://aolsvc.travel/aol.com.

———, "French Polynesia: History and Culture." http://aolsvc.travel/aol.com.

———, "Kiribati: History and Culture." http://aolsvc.travel/aol.com.

———, "New Caledonia: History and Culture." http://aolsvc.travel/aol.com.

———, "Vanuatu: History and Culture." http://aolsvc.travel/aol.com.

Maori, "Maori Culture." www.maori.org.

Maori Independence Site, "Maori Independence." http://aotearoa.wellington.net.nz.

Papua New Guinea Online, "History." www.niugini.com.

———, "People and Cultures." www.niugini.com.

Polynesian Islands, "French Polynesian History." www.polynesianislands.com.

Polynesia, Melanesia, Micronesia, "Who Do the Terms Mean?" www.concentric.net.

Tahiti, "About Tahiti." www.tahiti.com.

Index

Picture Credits

Cover Photo: © Eye Ubiquitous/CORBIS

© Associated Press, AP, 15, 63, 86

© Bettmann/CORBIS, 58, 65, 70, 71

© CORBIS, 73, 74

© COREL Corporation, 11, 16, 19, 22, 24, 25, 26, 28, 29, 30, 31, 34, 35, 37, 38, 39, 41, 44, 48, 56, 66, 78, 80, 82

Jeff DiMatteo, 12, 14, 55

© Jack Fields/CORBIS, 18

© Hulton-Deutsch Collection/CORBIS, 62

© Wolfgang Kaehler/CORBIS, 51

© Earl & Nazima Kowall/CORBIS, 85

© Danny Lehman/CORBIS, 53

© Charles and Josett Lenars/CORBIS, 83

© Michael Maslan Historic Photographs/CORBIS, 60

© James A. Sugar/CORBIS, 33

© Michael S. Yamashita/CORBIS, 47

About the Author

Anne Wallace Sharp is the author of the adult book, *Gifts*, a compilation of hospice stories, and four children's books, *Daring Women Pirates* and three others for Lucent Books, *The Inuit, The Blackfeet* and *Indigenous People of Australia: The Aborigines*. A retired registered nurse, she also has a degree in history. Her interests include writing, reading, traveling, and spending time with her grandchildren, Jacob and Nicole. Sharp lives in Beavercreek, Ohio.